PASSING BY

BOOKS BY JERZY KOSINSKI

NOVELS
The Painted Bird
Steps
Being There
The Devil Tree
Cockpit
Blind Date
Passion Play
Pinball
The Hermit of 69th Street

NONFICTION
(under the pen name of Joseph Novak)
The Future Is Ours, Comrade
No Third Path

JERZY KOSINSKI

PASSING BY

SELECTED ESSAYS, 1962–1991

Grove Press
New York

These essays have been previously published in *American Photographer, The American Scholar, The Boston Sunday Globe Focus, The Bulletin of the American Society of Newspaper Editors, Centaur, Crans-Montana Sporting Life, Dialectics & Humanism, Esquire, Life, Media & Methods, Minnesota Daily,* New York *Daily News,* New York magazine, *The New York Times, Paris Match, Polo, Time, U.S. News & World Report, Vanity Fair, Vineyard Gazette, Vogue, The Wall Street Journal,* and *The World Paper.*

Grateful acknowledgment is made to the following for permission to reprint previously published material:
THE NEW YORK TIMES: "The Reality Behind Words" by Jerzy Kosinski from October 3, 1971. Copyright © 1971 by The New York Times Company. Reprinted by permission.

First published in the United States of America in 1992 by Random House, Inc.
Grove Press paperback edition published in 1995

Published simultaneously in Canada
Printed in the United States of America

FIRST PAPERBACK EDITION

Library of Congress Cataloging-in-Publication Data

Kosinski, Jerzy N., 1933–1991
    Passing by: selected essays, 1962–1991/Jerzy Kosinski.—Grove
Press paperback ed., 1st paperback ed.
    "First published . . . in 1992 by Random House, Inc."—T.p. verso.
    Includes bibliographical references.
    ISBN 0-8021-3423-8
    I. Title.
PS3561.O8P388   1995   814'.54—dc20   95-19519

Grove Press
841 Broadway
New York, NY 10003

CONTENTS

ARTISTS AND EYE

THE SPORTY SELF

TALK OF NEW YORK

PEOPLE, PLACES AND ME

CONTENTS

SELF VS. COLLECTIVE

JEWISH PRESENCE

TIME OF LIFE, TIME OF ART

AFTERWORDS

ACKNOWLEDGMENTS

Jerzy had been working on this collection for some time prior to his death. He named and dedicated it, but was unable to complete his selections.

Therefore I should like to express my deep gratitude to Jerzy's and my friends Robert D. Loomis, vice-president and executive editor of Random House, and Dr. Byron L. Sherwin, vice-president of Spertus College of Judaica, for their personal encouragement, support, and professional judgment in the final preparation of this volume for publication. I know that Jerzy would join me in appreciation of their profound understanding of his work.

Mrs. Jerzy (Kiki) Kosinski

MOTTO

The principle of art is to pause, not bypass. The principles of true art is not to portray, but to evoke. This requires a moment of pause—a contract with yourself through the object you look at or the page you read. In that moment of pause, I think life expands. And really the purpose of art—for me, of fiction—is to alert, to indicate to stop, to say: Make certain that when you rush through you will not miss the moment which you might have had, or might still have. That is the moment of finding something which you have not known about yourself, or your environment, about others and about life.

1977

REFLECTIONS ON LIFE AND DEATH

ALEKSANDER
AND ANDRÉ WAT

I dedicated the "Notes of the Author on *The Painted Bird*" to André Wat. The "Notes" are important in that they originated as my correspondence about the German-language edition of *The Painted Bird* with my Swiss publisher. As a German-speaking Swiss, he had a complex attitude to them. I used to write to him from Paris, where I would sit with André Wat, talking about World War II.

I first met André Wat casually, while vacationing at Leba, Poland, in 1950, right after my matriculation.

I was passing by the Writers' Association House, a window was open, there was a party in progress. I went in and somebody said, "How are you, André," and introduced me around, saying, "This is the son of Ola and Aleksander Wat." So for the two days I spent in the house I was regarded as André Wat. Then, one day, a young man sat beside me and said, "How are you doing, André? How are the parents?"

"Everything's fine," I said. "Did they come?"

"Not yet, but they are coming soon," he said. "So I will introduce you to your parents, since I am sure you do not know them."

"What do you mean, I do not know my own parents?" I said.

"I do not know what your name is," he said, "but I am André Wat and they are my parents." And that is how we became friends.

André Wat's childhood was very traumatic. So much so that he did not even want to write about it. He left the task to his father, whose works he is restoring and publishing.

One day I told him, "André, I want to write novels, but as your father once told me to. How do I begin?"

André said, "Write a book that is most innocent and most depraved at the same time. Most innocent, because it will be about a child—about yourself, or me—but do it in sexual terms so that it is stirring; it is the only thing that makes a stir. Take a stand outside that process and try not to be alienated from it but, rather, be its presence and its absence at the same time— that is how the creative process happens."

André Wat was capable of summing up the creative process better than anyone else. So I asked, "What would move readers most?"

André said, "A child . . . we were all children once. It is a situation nobody can avoid. World War II and all those other facts are optional. But start with the child because, as a writer, you must be faithful to yourself first. Be faithful to your imagination. Think of what you could have seen if you had not seen what you saw. Think of what you saw during your wanderings, no matter where in Poland, and, if you can, turn this into an essential state of a child's endangerment, the greatest threat in history. If you can do it, you will have passed the test. Even if your English is bad and your imagination is all wrong, there will be one thing you will have in common with your readers. You will have written about a child. Everybody was a child."

Childishness is what we see in children. Children have an amazing ability for adaptation. Their adaptability grows out of their enormous imagination, as yet unspoiled and uncensored for its freedom of mental mobility. A child is capable of imagining anything. You can say to a child: Let us play a game. You are an angel and I will be the devil. The child will understand right away. That is something that stays with us. That element of freedom is the element of life. Childishness is a component of imagination. The point is, will that mind allow itself to go wild or won't it?

I have no family, no blood relatives. At this point I have no genealogical family. So I see the world in terms of friends. They are my family. In a sense, André Wat is my closest psychological brother. I think that he would very much want to gouge out the eyes of history, the history that had forbidden him to take his father's imagination to people in the country his father loved more than anything else.

For Aleksander Wat, Poland was the country of the mind. Poland was the country of sensitivity. It was a country suited for any kind of suffering, the burial ground of history our civilization had never experienced before and, at the same time, the site of most enjoyable cafés full of life. There is nothing wrong with cafés. Such cafés are not to be found anywhere else in the world. I speak from experience; after all, I am a café person. The café is a very important element of culture. My intellectual mentor, Professor Jozef Chalasiński, wrote about it. For a poet, for a writer, the café is the place where ideas are exchanged. It is a kind of philosophical Wall Street. Some shares go up, others fall. New stock is offered as intellectual enterprises are born and merge into conglomerates. For André Wat, Poland was a thought workshop; so it was for me too. For André Wat the important issue is whether the eyes of the Polish language will see the poetry of Aleksander Wat. Aleksander Wat is a poet of life and death. The lack of his poetry in the structure of Polish imagination means that the eyes are missing.

Aleksander Wat was constantly dying of psychological cancer. For many years he suffered from the most painful mental state known to man. His poetry was very precise; all unnecessary "stuff" was ironed out. It is the kind of poetry I will not call either difficult or easy, because poetry is like rock-and-roll: you either hear it or you do not. In Wat's poetry the essence of what life should be is crystallized, which is a clear confrontation between the cemetery and the incredible fullness of life. I have a poem which I always carry around to remind myself of what the language, reality, imagination and the consciousness of self are all about. It is called "A Lullaby for the Dying." It was written in Menton, France, in May of 1956. Wat mentioned it to me before I left for the United States.

When I feel like being hugged, when I feel like hugging, that is the instinct of life. One only needs to turn to a writer whose name is Wojtyla (Pope John Paul II), and read what Wojtyla has to say about love and responsibility. It is a very important book, with footnotes as significant as the main body of the text. In *The Hermit of 69th Street*, I go back to Wojtyla's footnote method. Love is an integral part of the love for the gift of life. The gift of life is unique. Being in love must lead to falling in love with life. The poetry of Aleksander Wat is not eroticized, which I notice because my writing is very erotic. Wat did not allow himself what I let myself enjoy: the sweep of devilish needs.

Aleksander Wat once sent me an essay he wrote about me, entitled "The Birth of a Poet." It was a very important message for me. In his essay, Wat turned his attention to what he never allowed himself: the wild desire to touch life physically. That was lacking in his poetry. There is the touching of the psyche— all his poetry was dedicated to the psychic side of life. Like Polish amber from the Baltic, he was a piece of amber with a special angle of refraction. His amber has a lot of the Baltic Sea in it, but it also has the Mediterranean, which gives it a different kind of light.

In my work it is the dramatic quality given to every single moment of life, including the present. I exist on many levels . . . one which involves me intensely; at the same time I am this man watching himself. Can I avoid it? I am very much in touch, I do not let myself be inert. I am very conscious. My alertness is the result of many things. World War II is one factor. This is my poetic part.

But I am also an actor. I do not want to be, because I was always scared of my own image and hated it. But I became an actor when a friend, Warren Beatty, persuaded me to play Zinoviev in the film *Reds*. And then I learned something incredible about myself, that I could be an actor while I was totally myself. I did not know how to act. Acting is a very serious occupation. You are not born an actor. As my father used to say, you must do a lot of sitting to get a job done right. Concentration is sitting, not talking. Ideas are a different matter. Acting, I learned I could be myself completely, say whatever I felt like saying. Do you know why? Because I do not care. What can be worse than what I remember from the past? So what counts? Only the state of consciousness and the state of being!

When I sat in an apartment where my mother died, I thought: Should I keep looking at her deathbed and at the books she used to read? Am I to regard myself as the victim of memories and tragedies? Or will I look at myself as the author of my own life, and tell myself: Listen, Kosinski. You are one lucky guy . . . who knows for how long. You received a very special gift from the country called Poland, in the center of Europe, in the center of culture. Face it. It is not as if I have not seen the world. Do I get bored in those other places? I do! Why? Because they do not have as much history, they were not taken apart as "we" were. That is "we" in the sense of the language. I say this as an American citizen. I am speaking about a psychological situation built around the dilemma: Is it going to be a state of mind based on life, or one immersed in shadows that my memory casts on my soul? Every single moment I face the dilemma: Shall I become like Auschwitz or like Kazimierz?* History offers both—an element of life and genius, and one of inertia and death. Aleksander Wat captured yet another element, one that I would not be able to pinpoint: the element of psyche animated by itself. Wat managed to overcome two things, the torture of life and the torture of physical suffering. If monuments were erected to the fullness of poetic life, the monument to Aleksander Wat would be among the most prominent.

I did not and will not go back to visit the villages I saw during the war, because what I have to say to myself and others I have already expressed in metaphors. I am not interested in explicit memory because I do not trust it. In my case memory is always clouded by my desire for inventiveness. I am no camera. I write because this is what makes me want to live. In the morning, as I face the typewriter, I also face myself and the threats of my memory, which tells me: Hey, watch out, or they will not like you. They will criticize you . . . they will say you are depraved . . . or too exotic . . . or you just pretend.

But I do not care, because I have survived and I am in a creative frenzy. Then a second voice tells me: OK, but you also need distance and control. Without control there is no self-knowledge. I gain control over what I do through language, the command of language that is sufficient to send signals to the reader. The language in my books is quite uncomplicated. Verbs and nouns in English are stronger than they are in Slavic languages. Each page I write tells me: Listen, Jerzy, try to see something you have not seen in your life or in the lives of others

*The old Jewish quarter next to Cracow.

around you. By talking to myself I also talk to my reader. Look at this. Read this poem by Aleksander Wat, "A Lullaby for the Dying." Aren't we all dying? Remember, the gift of life will not last forever. You also have this other option: "To long, under a bent cross, for what . . ."

1989

In our nation of 220 million, over 20 million have barely achieved functional literacy and over 80 million find reading too difficult to term it rewarding. Yet I feel that if those who almost never read for pleasure came to do so, their sense of fulfillment would be overwhelming.

This thought returns to me constantly as I indulge a particular passion, a series of voyages of personal discovery.

In recent years I use some of my free time reserved for walks and wanderings about the city—any city that I happen to be in or passing through—for visiting, usually late at night, a hospital's ward for the incurably ill, a nursing home for the aged, any refuge for those whom the world has discarded.

Once inside, I ask for the doctor in charge, the chief nurse, or the guard on duty. I introduce myself as a man in transit, still healthy, sportsman even, but first and foremost a writer—a novelist, a teller of stories, stories about men and women, children and adults, tales I would read gladly or recount to the one who, at such a late hour, is lonely, or abandoned or ignored—anyone who cannot sleep and might care to listen.

From the pocket of my raincoat I take out the hardcover

jacket of my most recent book, the photograph of my face on its inside flap, the only meaningful passport I carry.

My credentials established, I am then escorted through corridors and lobbies to a post between the oxygen tanks, the kidney machines, X-ray units, the grotesque armory of offerings enlisted in the defense of what is least defensible and most vulnerable—life in its evanescence, flesh in decay, beyond healing, a cancer in the innards of time, death having dispatched the pungent scent of mortality, its discreet calling card.

This is the regency of pain, undisputed by knowledge, numbed or stupefied by drugs, the unstoppable tide of television's images—once a transient folly, now no longer a distraction—the mere presence and voice of a visitor a ritual in useless name, one's own imagination the only messenger of consolation.

Intent on the shape before me—a man, a woman, a child—not to be cured, but breathing still, thought alive, I introduce myself as a traveler with time and inclination to spare, eager to meet one who is, like me, still traveling though on a different path. Settling on a chair, I begin to read a story from a novel of my own, or from a book of another author, always careful to keep my own presence in check so as to allow the language to release without hindrance the imagination of my listener.

My story now takes my listener along the trail of life, the trail painful, often surprising, but never as painful or as surprising as life in this room. Our visions unleashed, my listener and I now travel with the freedom unmatched by any spaceship over the mutable landscape of time lived, or left behind, or still to come, of revengeful wars, of nature that freely gave and fiercely took back of man's greed and man's mercy, of the strategies of love and deceit, of joy and despair. The stage is all set for the play of passion for one for whom passion is no longer a play, for whom life has lost fascination and allure, mystery and enigma.

No longer solitary, my listener is now like me, a fugitive, a displaced person in an uncharted landscape, an émigré to the frontier beyond the very scope of life's transit; with life about to end, an inner journey has only begun.

Jerzy Kosinski wrote this article for the thirtieth anniversary of the National Book Award in 1979. His novel Steps *won the award for fiction in 1969.*

DEATH IN CANNES

This story is not a tribute to death. Like birth, death is final; that's quite a tribute already. This story pays tribute to life. By the time it ends, life becomes visible only to the one who's about to die. Take a look at the picture of one such man. He is the one on the right in each picture. He is a man who knows that he will die—not eventually, as everyone does, but in a matter of days. The man on the left in each picture considers the older man his closest friend. He knows his friend is about to die— which, in a language a friend must not speak, means he's about to drop dead. Now that you know what each of them knows, picture them walking together through the busts and bustle of the Cannes Film Festival.

"In Hollywood," jokes the older man, "they would cast me as Conrad's Razumov, Dostoyevsky's Raskolnikov, or Kuprin's Romashov." Saying this, he knows that in Russian *razum* means "mind," that *raskol* means "dissent," and that Romashov dies in a senseless duel over a senseless love. Such facts of life are the elements of great literature. They were also the elements of this man's life. But since they cannot be learned from these (or any other) pictures, I'm not at all sure this story should be illustrated by them.

"Still, thanks for the pictures. They say a picture is worth a thousand words."

They say it, but they know this isn't true. They know that in order to be moved by an image (even as pure and commanding as image—the arabesque—is in Islam) you need to treat it with words (even if you're an Arab). They know that you move an image by giving it first a motive (and making it emotive), then by setting this motive in motion (a motion called emotion). And even in Cannes, a town of gamblers, still-life painters, and the Festival itself, they know that every motion picture begins by being treated in words—a treatment (even mistreatment)—in which every word is worth at least a thousand pictures.

To go on with this story, look again at these two pictures. They show two men on a sofa—hardly a still-life picture show. In one of the pictures both men seem to be smiling; in the other they appear to be sad—quite a change of mood, particularly since both pictures were taken within seconds of each other. So what? By themselves, these pictures can't even tell you whether they were taken with photographic art in mind, or a family album; whether they were taken for posterity or for a poster. By themselves they say nothing—not even which picture was taken first.

"I bet the smiling picture was taken last. I always bet on a happy ending."

You lost your bet. The "happy ending" picture was taken first. Paradoxically, it was taken after one of these two men (the one on the left) said something about a "happy ending," putting the stress on the word *happy*. He did this not because he is, by nature, a happy man (his nature happens to be gloomy—so gloomy that I bet in a Hollywood movie they would cast him as

Zinoviev, Lenin's "Comrade Gloomy"). He did this not because
he believes in happy endings (he doesn't: he believes that when
happy things end, their ending is unhappy). He stressed *happy*
because he could not possibly bring himself to stress the word
ending, and for this there was a good reason: for a long time, he
had thought of this man as his alchemical friend. The alchemical
friend is one in whom the image of one's father fuses with the
picture of one's best pal. Enough said. The moral: look at the
pictures if you must, but, even in Cannes, don't bet on them.
Bet on the worth of a word.

"Nevertheless, since you use pictures, is this piece nonfiction?"
    It isn't. This piece is about memory, and since memory is
fiction, call it autofiction. Autofiction (or "eye to I," as it is
sometimes called) is a literary genre, generous enough to let
the author adopt the nature of his fictional protagonist—not the
other way around. In this piece, the first and last name of the
man on the left of each picture are synonymous with the author's
name. To avoid confusing the two, call him JK.
    To get the true picture, mark the time. Both photographs
were taken on Thursday May 27, 1976, sometime, say, between
9:06 P.M. and 9:09 P.M. Now, since it's all in the name (and
not in the picture), mark the name of the gray-haired man: his
name is Jacques Lucien Monod. He is a man marked first by
birth—that is, by his name (a well-known name even if you
don't know it)—second by good looks (take a good look at his
pictures), and third by death, which a few months earlier paid
him its first visit disguised as hemolytic anemia. Now look him
up in *Who's Who in the World to Come*—a Who's Who particular
enough to list in its entries only those who stay alive even though
they have died; those whose names are always written in capital
letters—letters usually reserved for newspaper headlines.
    The Monod entry will tell you that like every mortal, he was

born not by his own design, but rather (as he would put it) by chance, in Paris and on February 9, 1910. Those who don't believe in chance, among them the numerically minded cabalists, will tell you that the presence of two number nines in Jacques's date of birth indicates that he was destined to be creative, and his birthday was a date—if only a blind one—with history. In other words, that his destiny was written for him in the stars long before he himself became one.

Further, it will tell you that Jacques's father, Lucien, a French Huguenot, was a well-known painter and a philosopher to whom Darwin was an idol, and that Sharlie Todd MacGregor, Monod's mother, was, in Monod's words, "a Milwaukee puritan revolutionary enough to leave Protestant America, settle in Catholic France, and marry an evolutionist." When Jacques was seven years old, he moved with his parents to Cannes, "a stone—a chip rather—away from the casinos of Nice and Monte Carlo," as he once remarked. In Cannes, Jacques grew up in a family home appropriately named Clos Saint Jacques (and apparently so named before the house was to cloister Jacques, the future "architect of molecular biology").* After passing his baccalaureate in Cannes, Jacques—already a young laureate of science—bypassed Cannes and went to study biology in Paris. Ever afterward, he would come back home to sail out on his boat, which he anchored in the Old Port of Cannes. *Tara* was his last boat.

The entry will tell you that Odette Brühl, Monod's wife (they married in 1938), was Jewish and "most refined. Refined as only a fine stone could be." Monod once described her that way, stressing the word *stone* possibly because Odette (who died four years before him) was an archaeologist and museum curator. The entry will tell you that Monod (whose godmother was mar-

*André Lwoff and Agness Ullmann, eds., *Origins of Molecular Biology: A Tribute to Jacques Monod* (Academic Press, 1979).

ried to Claude Debussy) played cello in a quartet so well that, back in 1936, he was offered a position as a symphony conductor but turned it down in favor of pursuing science ("or was it Odette?" he once suggested). It will tell you that during the war Monod was a member of the Communist-backed French Résistance and one who (quite by chance) escaped the grip of the Gestapo; that after the war, and not by chance, he resisted the Communist party, the very party he and Albert Camus (Monod's friend) once momentarily embraced. ("We merely hugged it," Monod would undoubtedly say here.) It will tell you that in 1965 Jacques Monod won the Nobel Prize for Medicine and Physiology (a prize he shared with André Lwoff and François Jacob). That from 1971 he was until his death in 1976 head of the Institut Pasteur ("Pasteur's pastor" as he called it), one of the world's most formidable bastions of medical research. You will also learn that Monod was a human-rights activist who came to the rescue of dissident scientists and that he spoke most fervently in favor of legalization of abortion in France and of euthanasia. You will learn that Monod was a mountain climber (this in spite of the polio he suffered as a boy), that he was utterly bilingual, that—oh, what the hell!—remember Monod but forget the Monod entry. Just keep in mind that however predestined he was, he believed only in chance, not in destiny. He wrote:

"*Against this notion, this powerful feeling of destiny, we must be constantly on guard. Immanence is alien to modern science. Destiny is written concurrently with the event, not prior to it.*"*

Because he also believed that "our number came up in the Monte Carlo game. Is it any wonder if, like the person who has

* Jacques Monod, *Chance and Necessity: An Essay on the Natural Philosophy of Modern Biology*, translated by Austryn Wainhouse (Alfred A. Knopf, 1971).

just made a million at the casino, we feel strange and a little unreal?" (1971), he was not surprised when (by chance) his book, *Chance and Necessity*, and *Being There* (a novel by JK about a man called Chance) were published simultaneously. Nor when an American book reviewer who didn't know the two were friends by chance wrote a review called "Monod and Kosinski: leaving it to Chance."

Now mark again the time: these pictures were taken at a reception in Cannes on Thursday evening. By Monday, 12:45 A.M., Jacques Monod would be headlines: JACQUES MONOD: ARCHITECT OF MOLECULAR BIOLOGY DIES IN CANNES AT SIXTY-SIX. THOUGHT EXISTENCE IS BASED ON CHANCE.

Watching Monod's face through the viewfinder of his camera, JK searches for signals of disaster, but all he finds are signals of joy. Eros and Thanatos get their signals crossed again.

"What excites you about women most?" asks JK.

"They carry life," says Monod, raising his eyes to JK. "They love life instinctively."

"And you love them—" JK hesitates.

"Instinctively," says Monod. Instinctively, he places his hand on the knee of the woman—a lively young lady to whom, by chance, he was introduced a moment before.

"Why are you in Cannes?" the lady on Monod's left asks him.

"I'm spending my vacation here," he says, leaning to her attentively, not hesitating on the word "vacation."

"For how long will you stay in Cannes?"

"I guess three, maybe four days," he answers almost absent-mindedly. "Too bad that then my vacation will be over." Until now, he would never have spoken of his life as a vacation. He smiles at her. The smile is a pretext. A Protestant at heart, he's a shy man. This is his way of looking at her.

———

"Two, maybe three days of life left. You'll ask incredulously, 'How can he be so sure?' "

Sure he can be sure. He can because, as JK knows only too well, Monod hasn't been feeling well for quite some time. He can because he is a medical man as well as a scientist. He can because he knows his disease has a six-month survival time tag attached to it, and that the six months are up.

"If things are as bad as you picture them so far, tell us exactly what makes Monod smile in that very first picture?"

What makes him smile is a phrase JK, looking around the room, utters at approximately 9:01. "Admit it, Jacques, paradoxically, all this makes for a pretty happy ending." (Monod himself used the word "paradoxically" very often.) The impact of "this"—here "this" stands for an entire life—reaches Jacques a full second later. He begins to smile, and that's when the photographer trains her camera on him.

"Now tell us what makes Monod sad? So sad that he practically averts his eyes in the second picture?"

It is what Monod says. He says: "Indeed, it's a happy ending." He stresses the word "ending"—a word that makes both men sad. That's when the photographer takes the second picture.

To understand further what takes place in all these pictures first picture Monod and JK, in Monod's apartment in Paris, a few weeks earlier.

"How was your condition finally diagnosed?" asks JK. He knows only that Monod has been ill.

"Finalement, it was diagnosed by Dr. Horace Bianchon as final as a *condition humaine,"* says Monod. Horace Bianchon was the M.D. who did medical wonders in *The Human Comedy.*

"Don't you find it touching that when the fifty-one-year-old Balzac was about to die he called for Bianchon, screaming, 'If Bianchon were here, he would save me!' " Monod pauses, then asks, "Would you like to come to Cannes too, for a week or so?" He stresses *a week or so*.

"I certainly would," says JK. "By chance, this will be the week of the Cannes Film Festival. Just think of all the festivities you will miss by sailing out on *Tara*!"

"This time I won't be sailing out," says Monod. "This time the boat and I will stay in Cannes."

"Wait, wait! Are you, in this piece, quoting Monod verbatim? Are these Monod's very words?"

As I said, this is autofiction. Monod's words are quoted in *autolingua*—the inner language of the storyteller.

Now picture Monod and JK (with Monod at the wheel) driving in Cannes on the way to that reception. JK knows how long the drive will last. He does not know how long Monod will.

"How long will you stay in Cannes?" asks JK while the car passes along the green golf course of the Cannes Country Club—one of the four local golf courses.

"Cannes is a paradox," says Monod, dismissing the question. "It has four golf courses! All those greens! In a French town! In France, practically nobody plays golf!" he exclaims. "Did I ever tell you I am color-blind, can't see green, and instinctively hate golf? No wonder that when I first read in *The Great Gatsby*, 'Gatsby believed in the green light, the orgastic future that year by year recedes before us,' I instinctively didn't like what I read!" He stops his car on a red light, then takes off the second the light changes to green.

"How long will you stay in Cannes?" JK asks again.

"As long as it will take for my red blood cells to turn green," says Monod. "By the way," he points at some house on the

route. "Maupassant stayed there," he says. "He used to sail to
Cannes on *Bel Ami*—his boat. He loved her as if she were a woman. It was he who first described the sky over Cannes as *'un ciel théâtral.'* Doesn't *ciel théâtral* sound better than 'dramatic sky'?" He speeds up and, climbing the hill, passes and bypasses by an inch a truck full of French military police. "Did you know that Maupassant—that *pauvre bel ami*—died of syphilis—and that he died mad from it—and at forty-three? Imagine him, a man who loved women more than life, dying of syphilis—at the time this was an incurable disease and one that, by ravaging the lovers, gave love itself a bad name. Think of him, of the most rational of French naturalist writers, dying mad—not even knowing that he was dying, that his time had come, that he, a man who wrote 'Le Horla'—still the best story about going mad—would one day die mad!" He slows down at a turn, then speeds up again. For a moment the car skids, and so does Monod behind the wheel. JK panics. "The car went out of control, not I," Monod reassures him.

"By what name would Horace Bianchon call your condition today?"

"Today, he'd call it hemolytic anemia."

"Is this the one you first mentioned when you spoke to me about it last December?" JK tries again.

"Did I?" Monod grins. "Well, if I did, I bet you promptly looked it up in your portable *Materia Medica*." He laughs. He has seen JK do this before—but only when it was for his own *maladies imaginaires*. He laughs. "Did you?" he asks, examining his tanned face in the car's rearview mirror. Color his skin waxy pale and his tan yellow.

"I did," JK admits.

"Did the *Materia Medica* say anything about what happens when the conversion of bilirubin to bilirubin glucoronide exceeds the liver's capacity to excrete it into the bile?"

"It did," says JK. "It spoke of considerable changes in brown skin pigmentation, which—only in Cannes!—could safely pass for a tan."

"What else did it say?" Monod examines him offhandedly.

"It said something about the shortened life of one's red blood cells; about the bone-marrow production no longer keeping up with massive destruction of RBCs. Something about a rather simple criterion by which the progress of the disease can be measured day by day, as well as time—the number of days—still left to a patient," says JK, putting stress on *time*. "It spoke about acute hemolytic crisis, about sudden trembling and shaking—the beginning of sudden shock and prostration—the signs of an imminent end." JK watches Monod's hand on the wheel. The steering wheel trembles. The trembling comes either from a bad road or poor shock absorbers—not from Monod.

"While you studied *Materia Medica*, I received some medical advice from Seneca," says Monod. "When it comes to helping a terminal case—that is, the case of every one of us—he's still the best doctor in the business. By the way: Did you know that Seneca was the first well-known vegetarian? That, at one time or another, he treated Descartes, Corneille, Rousseau, Diderot and Balzac, as well as Queen Elizabeth I? That Emerson included Moses, John and Paul, Shakespeare *and* Seneca in his portable bible?"

He slows down the car to take a look at someone's historic home. "Gérard Philippe, the movie star, who died so young, was born here!" he says, then picks up speed.

"What did Dr. Seneca say?" Faced with the inescapable, JK becomes stoic.

"He said, 'C'mon, *mon cher* Monod, are you reluctant to leave things undone, unfinished, incomplete? Well, don't be. You're leaving nothing undone, because there are no fixed number of sacred duties laid down for us to complete—surely you know that dying is also one of life's sacred duties. Every life is a short one, and no matter how sacred, it is not to be bought at all costs. What matters is not how long it is, but how good it is. End it anywhere—just make sure that you end it with a happy ending.' "

"But it doesn't have to end," says JK, who can't bring himself to exchange "it" for "your life." "What I read in *Materia Medica* stressed the need of multiple transfusions." He pauses. Call his pause a thoughtful intermission. "How many transfusions do you still need?"

"Before I become a still life?" Monod grins. "At least two a week."

"When will you have your next one?"

"There won't be a next one."

"You mean you've recovered?"

"Only from the shock. The shock of my last transfusion."

"If no more transfusions—then what? Won't you eventually have to be attached to some sort of a time machine? When?"

"There will be no time machine," says Monod.

"Why not?"

"Mercy killing interests me; mercy living does not."

"*All the traditional systems have placed ethics and values beyond man's reach. Values did not belong to him; he belonged to them. He now knows that they are his and his alone, and they no sooner come into his possession than lo! they seem to melt into the world's uncaring emptiness. It is then that modern man turns toward science, or rather against it, finally measuring its terrible capacity to destroy not only bodies but the soul itself.*" (Monod, 1971)

"You're only sixty-six. This is your intellectual prime," says JK. "If it weren't for just this damn bad blood you would be in tip-top shape. Given all you've done for medical science—as well as for the pharmaceutical industry—won't science and the industry give you the best time machine there is? A machine that could give you time to finish *Man and Time*, your next book?" He stresses *next*.

"Man and time, not man and machine," says Monod. "Besides, had there been such a machine—I'm not sure there is—and had I let myself be attached to it, would they ever let me die?" He stresses *they* but doesn't say who "they" are. "I can already see the headlines in *France-Noir* [he puns on *France-Soir*] in the year 2010. THE HEAD OF JACQUES MONOD IS A HUNDRED YEARS OLD TODAY AND STILL RUNNING PASTEUR. HAPPY BIRTHDAY IRON MASK!" Tires screeching, he takes a sharp turn. "I would rather be MONOD CANNED AT THE FESTIVAL IN CANNES." He makes his own headline, then stops the car at the curb and turns off the engine. They are on top of Cannes. The spectacular panorama of still life opens below. Monod glances toward the Boulevard du Midi, then at the Croisette. At the Palais des Festivals, then at the Palm Beach Casino—the veritable Doges' Palace devoted to dodging chance.

"A Soviet critic once insinuated that my antideterminism and my anti-Marxist stand on chance, as he put it, stemmed not from my ethics or knowledge, not from my lab at Pasteur, but from my growing up in Cannes—the capitalist casino town." He looks toward the horizon, toward the island of Ste. Marguerite. He scans the bays of La Napoule and Golfe Juan, then looks toward the horizon. He is not looking at Cannes. He is looking at his life.

"Did you know that the Man in the Iron Mask was kept in the fort on the island of Ste. Marguerite? Paradoxically, the mask was made of velvet. This is the same fort in which six Huguenot pastors were once kept in solitary confinement until their death. All but one went mad—and the one who didn't spent thirty years there! Think of spending thirty years in solitary confinement!" He is not speaking of solitary confinement. He is speaking about a time machine.

He starts the car's engine, listens to an unruly knock, then engages the reluctant transmission and takes off, losing the race to two sports cars flanking him.

"Wait, wait. Tell us about Monod's car. Like the French, we Americans are a car-loving nation. Our love affair with a car kills some fifty thousand Americans every year and maims for life God knows how many. Tell us at least what sort of car Monod was driving? Was his car as classic as he?"

It was not.

"Let me try again. Monod was clearly an open-minded man. Was his car a convertible—which in French is called décapotable *(the word that rightly could stand for 'capable of decapitation')."*

Monod's car was a two-door sedan. It opened no more than did Monod. You see, Monod opened himself to you the way a book does: one page at a time. It could have been a page about microbiology. Or about literature. Or about sailing. Or (I grant you this) one devoted to his car. To any car. Monod was a scientist: the car's mechanical ingenuity—primarily its motor—interested him most. To him, driving was simply motoring.

"This is all very interesting, but finally tell us what car Monod drove during the last days of his life?"

It was, I think, a rental—a car Monod might have rented in Cannes. This time, before coming to Cannes, Monod left his own car (a Porsche, by the way) in Paris.

"How did you leave your things when you left Paris?" JK asks Monod.

"The way I found them the day before—and before. And before," says Monod. "You might say last week I walked out of my garden the way your Chance did out of his."

"What time do you have?" asks JK.

"Enough to enjoy the rest of the weekend," Monod replies with a smile.

They drive along the highway. Monod slows down. "Did you know that Prosper Mérimée prospered here?" He points at someone's home, then negotiates an uphill turn. The negotiations fail. The car skids, then, on a straight, comes to a short stop. Monod lurches forward and so does the passenger. JK panics again.

"It's only a stop sign." Monod laughs. "Their sign—not mine." Tires screeching, he takes off and he speeds up all the way to the reception. They arrive on time.

Now, with no pictures to assist you, picture a sprawling villa situated high above Cannes (and well above most people's situation). Outside picture a stream of limos and streamlined sports cars. Inside picture a motion-picture crowd—all in motion. Here, the four-star Hollywood stars mingle freely with the French *vedettes*—and the assorted lovers of cinema.

As Monod and JK make their way through the rooms looking for a place to sit down, the French crowd recognizes Monod and ogles him with deference, while the Americans here know he must be a star (he is so handsome, so at ease, so tanned) but they don't know in which movie he last played.

"Who is he?" an L.A. Century City male asks, pointing his little finger at Monod.

"Someone said he played in a movie called *Chance and Necessity*," his Sunset Stripper tells him.

"Did anyone tell you, you could be a Charles Boyer?" A Rodeo Drive madam accosts Monod.

"Charles Boyer did," says Monod.

Attention is contagious: within seconds the Americans crowd Monod. Star-struck, they still don't know their star. Their star is a meteor. In a matter of days, the meteor will crash.

The last day. Late afternoon. On the terrace of Monod's home, Monod and JK face each other. JK takes pictures of

Monod. In between, to interrupt the picture-taking ritual—the purpose of these pictures is to preserve Monod—JK clowns for him. In the picture of the two of them photographed by a mutual woman friend, JK reenacts for Monod a man who, about to be shot by a firing squad, still combs his hair.

Offhandedly, Monod picks up a pack of cigarettes. Offhandedly he takes out a cigarette. Offhandedly he lights it, and offhandedly he draws on it. This is the first time JK has seen Monod doing anything offhandedly. The reason he does it is that his hand is trembling—he is trying to be offhanded about it.

"How do you feel?" asks JK.

"I feel so-so," says Monod. "I really shouldn't smoke," he says offhandedly. "I guess this will be my last cigarette. What will you do tomorrow?" he asks.

"I will go to the beach."

Monod keeps smoking his cigarette. Suddenly, in the viewer of his single-lens 35mm reflex camera, JK sees Monod's cigarette trembling. In a single reflex he focuses the lens more closely. Does the trembling come from the photographer or from his camera? Does it come from Monod or from his cigarette? He focuses and refocuses again and again. There is no doubt that the trembling—a trembling that borders on shaking—comes from Monod, and that even though he is aware of it, Monod cannot stop it. He—a master of control—cannot control the trembling of his hand. He can only camouflage it—and he does this first by smoking a cigarette, then by immobilizing his hand on the arm of his chair. Then, as JK keeps on viewing Monod through the lens, Monod's eyes become blurred. Blurred as if by moisture settling on the lens. JK focuses his lens more closely. The drops in Monod's eyes come from Monod, not from the humidity. Call them tears.

"Tell me, Jacques, are you afraid?" asks JK who, asking this, can no longer focus his camera as moisture forms in the camera's eyefinder. The moisture comes from his eyes.

"Afraid? Why afraid?" asks Monod. He is a proud man. Proud men don't cry. To hide his tears, he turns toward the sun and he smiles in its face. This, by the way, will be his last smile. Soon, he will get up, extend to JK his hand and, after their last handshake, he will say, "Farewell, my dear boy!" and enter the house for the last time. (The door to the house is already open.)

But now, moments before that final moment, he looks toward the sun setting over Cannes, over *un ciel théâtral*, and he smiles. His smile is as radiant as the sun. It is a smile of Sisyphus who, staring Death in the face, sees nothing but the sun. It is a joyful smile of one who is "contemplating the series of unrelated actions which becomes his faith, created by him, combined under his memory's eye and soon sealed by his death." Albert Camus saw him that way in the brief episode Monod quoted as an epigraph to *Chance and Necessity*. It begins with "At that subtle moment when man glances backward over his life . . ." and ends with "One must imagine Sisyphus happy."

1986

LIFE AND ART

ON BOOKS

Books remain the most important means of expression because books are democratic in that they grant readers the freedom to interpret their meaning, unlike paintings, which, in a way, impose their meanings on their viewers. A book, like a culture, says to its reader: My dear, I'm yours. You are free to do with me what you will. I am your entrance into yourself and into history at the same time.

1989

When I was accused of perhaps being the devil incarnate, I answered that I thought I am more the embodiment of an angel—if we agree that childhood means growing into the world of control and oppression. One is a child when others are already grown up—that is a state of war, a state of endangerment. Children see the world from a different angle. The lens of a child's mind is closer to the earth and captures things from below . . . this might be the source of our devilishness. But, in a sense, childhood is also an angelic state, because of the suffering.

When you try to remember your own childhood, it is hard to recall your thoughts as a child. You do not remember your sixth year, or your seventh or eighth year. What you do remember are certain versions that have been condensed and defined by your mind as an adult. Children do not register things or, rather, if they do, they do it in their own childish language, which is like a telegram without content. Children's drawings tell more. Look at the pictures drawn by children under the German occupation of Poland. The pictures are trying to say incredible things! If the children were able to express all this in words, what kind of a novel would it make? As a child, what story could

I have told? Could I have competed with newsreels of World War II? It is inconceivable! Could Aleksander Wat have done it? Could André Wat? Could anybody express the drama of death in a different, better way than Auschwitz did?

When it is said that the world is without order, they are talking about its metaphysical structure. There is an order to the world, an order of a spiritual kind. There is no need to ask who gave it to us. We must cherish the gift, which is called the gift of life and which arrives packaged as a baby. Who sent it? We must be very thankful to whoever did. We must pay a lot of respect to that gift, because it comes with a little note scribbled by the sender in Hebrew letters, in Christian script or in Islamic characters, saying, "This is a gift for you. You can do with it anything you want." It is more than a gift of life, it is a miracle of life. But there is another little note attached to it, in very small, indistinct print, that says, "You can lose this gift at any moment." For me, then, the world is a state of life.

In 1965 my first novel appeared, called *The Painted Bird*, and in Poland was declared offensive. I was cut off from my family by my own writing, by a book about a child, about the state of childhood and about the rebellion of imagination expressed in sexual terms. Was the writing shocking? Was it more offensive than World War II and all that happened in Poland under the Nazi occupation? In *The Painted Bird*, I was trying to apply the rules Aleksander Wat taught me when he said: "You must touch the reader because the reader will not be touched by history on its own. In your book, you must re-create the state of oppression that is present in the stories you tell. And remember, you will not be able to use gestures; nobody will hear your accent; they will not see your eyes or the agony you express with your body language. Everything must be contained in verbs, adjectives, nouns and adverbs. That is all you have. And we are not talking about relating history fact by fact; that would take millions of years. We are talking about print—print that must touch the reader's mind; print that, in itself, is nothing, ink on paper; printing technique that has not changed in almost a thousand years, since Gutenberg's Bible. That is all you have."

After all, in my books I do not write about any particular country called Poland or Greece or Yugoslavia, where children died by the millions. I do not write about Harlem, where children die too, because they lack a vision of life. Children die as they grow and later turn into living or dead adults. I write about a state of imagination that wants to tell you: Hear something for the first time, something shocking about yourself. What is it that offends you? Sexuality offends you? A story of a girl raped by several peasants?

We do not remember ourselves when we were six but we do remember the dramas of that age. I am made of many such dramas. In my adult life I am trying to transform them into something that will touch others, and that is my way of rewarding myself for my traumatic childhood. Could my childhood during World War II be anything but traumatic?

Even setting aside *The Painted Bird*—a book about a child; regard it as a book about the moon—how do you think a Jewish child could survive World War II? Whoever sheltered that child risked his or her own life as well as those of their family members. Concentration camp was the punishment for not reporting the child's whereabouts. My survival in Poland was like a generous credit. Those who sheltered me in Poland faced the death penalty. What kind of childhood did that produce? Traumatic, no question about it. I, the child, was responsible for the endangerment of adults. A child as an enemy in the history of World War II. Can one imagine a more traumatic experience? Try to imagine the dramatic repercussions this had on the child's mind. Of course I am carrying them in myself. My control over the language is from control I learned during World War II. As a child with a very Jewish appearance I struggled, from the very nature of life, to survive at any cost and not to expose those who helped me to the death penalty. I understood that in keeping me they were living on credit, as they did not know how long the war was going to last. Today we know that it lasted four and a half years. Those who sheltered me did not know whether it was going to last a week, two weeks, three, one year or five. What if somebody saw this strange, dark child—a child, not a rabbit, running across the country road. There will be a secret report. Why the report? Because, after all, we are living in the period of historical bloodbath. Nothing counts anymore. We are talking about morality during World War II. Death penalty for sheltering a child! You are asking me what effect World War II had on me.

Dramatic! Traumatic! Dramatic! That is exactly it! To turn trauma into drama, to show Auschwitz as the fullness of life. To sum up, World War II resides in me as a drama, as something to be narrated so that it touches others.

1989

THE REALITY
BEHIND WORDS

NEW HAVEN—

The American poet Chayym Zeldis once told me that the reason
he could do without certain things in life was that their names
produced unwelcome responses in him, believing, as I do, that
language is indeed the creator of reality when it gives a name to
it. But one does not have to be a poet or a novelist—or an
advertising sloganeer—to realize that words, like commanding
officers and their men, can massacre innocent bystanders; and
that often it is language that evokes in us a passion to embrace
or reject others, to love or kill, to be free or be confined.

Particularly if the hand holds a gun, we value words: we do
not kill, we "evacuate" or "waste"; we don't ship out bodies, we
"transport remains" home; and we don't fail, we "underachieve."

Especially when the hand clasps the credit card of commerce,
we don't care whether the words matter, permitting commercials and advertising to revise our imaginations daily without
the blink of an eye. In either case, imagine if you will this daily
scene in your friendly neighborhood courtroom peopled with the
judge, defendants, prosecutors, lawyers, jurors, and among the
audience, the impatient representatives of our friendly automobile insurance companies.

The case before the court: a multiple automobile crash on

your friendly neighborhood highway, which has caused a few
deaths, one or two dismemberments, and considerable property damage. All the defendants plead not guilty; they claim that just before the crash each of them was carefully driving his own friendly, properly registered, insured and recently inspected American-made motor vehicle. Their car models are called—as they are in actuality—Demon, Super Bee, Firebird, Tempest, Charger, Toronado, Centurion, Cutlass and Road Runner. The motor vehicles they inadvertently crashed into are named Thunderbird, Rebel, Cyclone, Swinger, Sting Ray, Dart, Barracuda and Fury. The accidents took place on a friendly community road called the expressway.

". . . and therefore, Your Honor, when I saw this man trying to pass by me on the right in his Challenger, sure I stepped on it. Why, my Boss, which I just bought . . ." protests one defendant.

"Objection, Your Honor. The car's name is irrelevant!" interrupts the prosecutor.

Should an objection against a name—a word—be sustained in this instance? Who but friendly defendants in most cases kill over fifty thousand friendly Americans yearly in car accidents on our friendly highways? Considering the pain, destruction and death these drivers caused, would it have been more appropriate if their four-wheel modes of transportation had been named by car makers from Detroit—as indeed they ought to be—Collider, Veerer and Catapulter (for the young crowd, of course); Relapser (for those who think young); Maimer (medium-priced range); Polluter (top of the line); Autopsy-Coupe 400 (limited edition); Annihilator, Waster and Evacuator (the last three models available to military personnel at no extra cost with protective camouflage paint); and the compact Off-Roader?

Would a man driving the economical Super-Wound Convertible, for instance, race a lady smiling from her ash-colored Vista-Paralyso? Would a citizen in a supercharged Cougar drag race against a couple of teenagers in their Wildcat, if instead he were driving a Custom-Disintegrator and they drove their parents' Hard-hat-Vapido? Of course not!

To my mind, a man proudly driving his Comet, Satellite or Galaxie is more than likely imaginatively to leave this friendly earth's orbit simply because the automobile's name makes him feel that he is driving some extraterrestrial vehicle.

Must our attitude toward the language continue to remain that ambiguous—or that fraudulent? Too frequently language manipulates us when we are unaware of our responses to it; yet when we are conscious of these responses we conveniently dupe ourselves by ignoring the language whenever it becomes threatening.

"Every individual or national degradation," Joseph de Maistre notes, "is immediately foretold by a strictly proportioned degradation in the language itself." Today our society is continually subverted by what is one of its greatest threats—monolithic, dictatorial Wordcon.

1971

WHERE AN AUTHOR
CAN BE HIMSELF

When I flew to New York yesterday from Europe I recalled
a similar trip that I made twelve years ago. In the decade
that has passed, not much has changed on the other side of
the Iron Curtain. But much has changed here in America.
Then I—perhaps more than others—saw America as a free
country.

I still see it that way—but it is a different America now.
It has become polarized, as Europe has been for centuries.
Americans are no longer the same. They are less anonymous.
They wrest freedom from each other. They clearly delineate
their places in society. They are angry, violent and abusive.
They have become political. And the system responds in turn
and invades their freedom.

Nevertheless, in terms of my life, the fact that I could write
my novel and have it published exactly as I want is of signifi-
cance.

Here, the appearance of a novel still remains spontaneous.
A book is born in privacy and often strikes back at society. Its
voice is heard. And it is you, all of you—publishers, editors,
critics and judges—who keep it so. This is what gives this award

particular importance. And because of what you are, a writer can remain himself. For this am profoundly grateful.

1969

Jerzy Kosinski's acceptance speech at the 1969 National Book Award ceremonies (for his National Book Award in Fiction for Steps)

OUR "PREDIGESTED, PREPACKAGED POP CULTURE" —A NOVELIST'S VIEW

Growing up in a Communist state, I was trained to become a "deliverer": an intellectual bureaucrat who delivered others to those destinies the state had defined for them. I refused to do that, starting at the age of twelve, when—rejecting my "destiny"—I would not put on a youth-movement official uniform I was given to wear.

When I came to this country, I could have taken up a number of professions—photographer, anthropologist or statistician—but I wanted to write, because fiction is a very democratic form for the conveyance of ideas. It identifies itself from the outset as fiction, not fact. That's a very democratic admission, informing the reader: "It's up to you. Take it or leave it. Project yourself into this situation or not."

Fiction doesn't seduce you by false promises. It doesn't guarantee to change or improve your life. It's the business of imagination that you as the reader and I as the novelist share while you are reading my book.

Fiction doesn't change anybody's life; it merely hints at different ways of looking at oneself, at others and at society. It may not change your life, but you may choose to go through it differently, exploring new philosophical, ethical and emotional options.

Fiction is a relatively marginal part of popular culture—that all-pervasive cultural climate basically molded to adolescent expectations. Popular culture makes little demand for sustained effort. It's predigested, prepackaged and calls for a minimal attention span.

Popular culture is typified by the enormous popularity of entertainment, television, films and radio that make great use of pop music—adolescent disco music. Since perceiving popular music doesn't call for our intellectual apparatus to be at work, one could say that the more of such entertainment we have around, the less we think.

Another growing trend that I see in popular culture is escapism. This is demonstrated by the popularity of science fiction that's neither science nor fiction. It is the ultimate form of escaping unchallenged from one's immediate environment.

What is happening around us takes the form of a curious mixture of the adolescent perception of society and of oneself. For example, a popular movie offers an oddly naïve interpretation of a community's life: its enemy as a giant shark. How many of us actually expect to be threatened by a shark? Life's challenges will not take place in the ocean!

I'm not contemptuous of popular culture—which has a place in a free society—but I have a right to counter it. For every sea shark of popular culture, I come up in my novels with a street shark—something that really exists.

I see myself as an adversary novelist whose role is to confront—not to escape from—life's threatening encounters. There is nothing in all my novels that couldn't take place in these United States in the very city block in which so many of us live.

The changing moral scene in America—the swinging scene,

the singles scene, for example—is nothing like its representation in most pulp writing, TV plays and the movies. Rather it reflects the great number of people who don't know what to do after having grown up in a society which basically leaves individuals to themselves, with all the options available to them.

Well, there are some options that perhaps we shouldn't take. We need spiritual guidelines to know which options are good and which bad. That's what literature has always done: It enlarges the world of emotional and ethical options. When you're finished reading a novel, you are stronger than when you started, though it may have made you feel pained or shocked.

There is another reason why imaginative fiction is so important in America:

It is because this is truly the last society which still modifies itself freely. In other words, you cannot predict what life will be like tomorrow in this country. You can in almost any other industrial country. You know what France, West Germany, Poland, Sweden or Switzerland will be like tomorrow.

But the United States has always been and is now in a state of what I would call a very healthy turmoil. It is a country in a state of permanent moral revolution. In such a country, people are caught in moral, sexual, physical dilemmas which neither they nor their parents or teachers could have foreseen even a few years ago.

A society which changes so quickly makes one obvious impact:

Like any other sudden change, it catches a lot of people unprepared. They're caught very often as victims. They feel baffled, they feel lost—and no "how to" book can help them. They are not emotionally strong enough to make decisions.

Decisions such as, for instance, whether to marry or whether to abandon one's too expensive home or to look for another job all call for a summoning up of one's inner strength. The great value of a novel is that it provides an arena for mustering emotion, intellect and imagination—all needed when coming to a decision.

To read a novel is to practice for real life.

1979

T O   H O L D   A   P E N

*S*ome time ago I filed an application for a loan at one of the major New York City banks. Under the heading "profession," I wrote "writer." After I completed the application, one of the bank officials thrust it back at me. "You say you're a writer? Now, what do you really do?" he asked.

As a child, I wanted to be a writer because I thought writers knew everything: how a fly can walk up a wall, why the seven dwarfs had to work while Snow White sat at home and did nothing, and so on. In high school, my fascination with the craft of writing continued. What intrigued me most then was the writer's ability to transcend time. He controlled his characters forever; no revolution, no war could upset the balance of power between the writer and his creations. Later, when I attended universities in Poland and the Soviet Union, I became aware that an author's strength lies not in his omniscience or in his control over time, but in his ability to address and awaken his reader's consciousness. The growing number of silenced or imprisoned writers made Voltaire's *"Qui plume a, guerre a,"* immediately relevant: to hold a pen was indeed to be at continual, personal war. The persecutions impressed upon me the writer's potential as an intellectual, political and moral force, a force powerful enough to threaten a police state.

When I left Eastern Europe in 1957, then, I felt a writer to be a unique being, utterly grounded in the conditions of his present existence, but able—with the aid of the printing process—to project himself and his experiences into the future. While an engineer is confined to working with steel and concrete, and may expect his bridge to rust or decay or perhaps be replaced by another bridge more suitable to future society, a writer, confined to the limits of his imagination and of words, is less subject to temporality. His product will be passed on to the future in exactly the same form in which it first appears. His novels or poems or stories will never be redesigned. In fact, they will never be "finished," so long as they are being read; writing is a continual process of communication, which depends as much on the reader's ability to decipher the words as it does on the words themselves. A writer merely presents a framework of ideas, words and images in order to trigger the reader's imagination, but that framework itself is not the final goal; in order to be effective, writing has to transcend its physical properties. Thus, while an engineer must be entirely accountable for his bridge and may be judged a success or failure on the basis of its stability and aesthetic appeal, a writer's work can never be approached in terms of its surface appearance or functionality. Furthermore, since the only true measure of literature's effectiveness is the extent to which the reader's awareness is expanded, the writer's ultimate success or failure can never be entirely known.

Because of the basic nonutilitarian nature of writing, a novelist becomes something of an anomaly in a culture that prizes usefulness and efficiency. It would have been easier for the bank official to accept me, for instance, if I had been an engineer. Yet I have come to expect precisely his reaction since I began writing fiction in America. While Europe's political development constantly assumed her writers' innate political influence, American writers have seldom been considered political threats. Rather, they have been treated as superfluous characters, more interested in publicizing their private experiences and fantasies than in galvanizing political emotion. This attitude toward writing may be explained in part by the traditional American mistrust of novelists. Because the creation of literature is not often the means to financial success and security, is not aimed at any tangible object, and requires no special training—all important aspects of American commercialism—writing fiction is seldom considered a serious endeavor. A novelist is simply another self-styled elitist.

1973

A   S E N S E   O F   P L A C E

L ike other participants of this literary gathering,* I was asked
to read my piece on a sense of place in three minutes—with
three minutes representing about two and a half double-spaced
pages, and not my own clearly timeless sense of place.

Now, as you know, in our era of television, three minutes is
a very long time.

I recall the last leader of South Vietnam, whose country had
just fallen to the enemy, when, as a guest on a nationally televised American TV talk show, he was asked by the talk show
host:"Tell us, sir, what went wrong in South Vietnam? We have
a whole minute for your answer!" Calmly, the South Vietnamese
leader answered, "We lost the war!"

Storytelling has been my chosen vocation—vocation, not vacation—inherited from the oral tradition of my people. Since my
high school days in Poland, my creative self has chosen writing
as my favorite all-terrain literary vehicle. This vehicle—call it
self-invention—is amphibian enough both to dive deep into my
deepest realms and also to fly me in the most remote regions of

---

*On the occasion of the celebration of the P.E.N./Faulkner award for
fiction. Washington, D.C., October 1, 1990.

fancy. Never stationary, it remains in a constant state of plight. Plight, not fight, since, depending upon being decoded by my readers, my sense of place as found in my novels remains apolitical, nonjudgmental and, like all fiction, thanks to its open-ended nature, nondidactic. Hence, democratic, my fictional craft is propelled by at least three pollution-free cultural fuels. One stems from a narrative tradition of one-on-one confession, so popular in Poland, a country where, first introduced to confessing as well as confessional fiction, I spent the first twenty-four years of my life. The second fuel is Hassidic, so high in narrative octane that it allows the storyteller unsurpassed freedom to probe any taboo-ridden territory. The third fuel comes directly from Thomas Jefferson's Memoranda (unfairly called *Autobiography* by his latter-day publishers) and, above all, from his immortal "all men are created equal," a statement which extends to the stories these men tell as being equally equal.

By now you might ask: Is there a specific place where my hermetic sense of place would like to pause? Yes, there is. With a photographic camera in hand, I would love to be seated in an old French horse-drawn cab for hire, the seat expressly created by Gustave Flaubert in *Madame Bovary* for Emma and her lover. As you know, the very first installment of *Madame Bovary* appeared today, on October 1 in *Revue de Paris*, but in the year 1856. However, that back seat simply isn't to be found in this very first installment of Flaubert's novel. Why not? Simple! The French publishers, acting as censors, removed the entire backseat passage from the novel's first installment. They did it because there, in the back of that hired cab, exercising Flaubert's right to his own sense of place, Emma and her lover, the two consenting adults, engaged in adulterous lovemaking, the very moment meant to evoke within us an additional dimension of our sense of place.

Those who write make assumptions for the rest of us, as if we are too dull to understand and that we in fact do not deserve to be informed about slightly more complex things. They write about the most elementary, idiotic things and then of course we read it and then they think, well, that is what they read, let them have more of that stuff, so it gets worse and worse.

Some of the scenes in my novels are triggered by something I have seen or maybe been part of. But that would be true of any novelist, even if he writes from extreme imagination. Imagination is still part of his head and his head is grounded in life.

In my fiction I write as factographically as possible. I try to involve the reader in something that creates a dramatic menace. It is menacing fiction. Art cannot be menacing unless it makes some reference to life. My endless rewriting—my trying to condense it, my trying to make it as quintessentially dramatic as only fiction can be—I think does something else also. In some ways it becomes morally dangerous. One of the elements of my fiction is that my characters defend themselves against oppressive circumstances. Occasionally, of course, they revert to revenge as a psychic defense. There is a great degree of treacherous behavior in my novels, and to say that I have written this straight from life in some way implies that I have done these things. It was not an accident that during one of my lectures a well-meaning listener got up and said, "Mr. Kosinski, how many men have you actually killed, Sir?" I said, "You mean in Europe or in this country?" He said, "In this country." I said, "In this country I cannot tell you because I would be still liable." The result is that people will not sit next to me at a dinner because they feel that clearly, if this man writes from life, what kind of life is this?

Not only do I make references to my own life and work, I make references to other imaginative works, but nobody picks these other signals up. They will pick up on my sedan. OK, big deal, so Kosinski also drives a car. Great autobiographical discovery. Is my car a Buick? "Yes." Is my character also driving a car? I say, "Yes, but maybe not a Buick."

Thank goodness novelists die, because their biographies die with them. So then you just read their books. You read *The Kreutzer Sonata* by Tolstoy and you no longer say, "Oh, Tolstoy knew this musician and this musician was making a pass at Tolstoy's wife." You do not know that . . . and any minute now I am going to get rid of my car too, so the critics are going to be totally dumbfounded. What will they write about now that Kosinski has no car? Without a car he is finished as a novelist.

In a way I begin to regret having written my two nonfiction books under the pen name of Joseph Novak. It was great fun at the time, because I could recommend these great books by Novak to everyone but nobody knew I wrote them. And no one would talk about the books in terms of my own life; they would have to analyze them for what they were.

Reading the reviews of my novel *Pinball*, I certainly consider writing under a pen name. I am going to write a novel so autobiographical about Kosinski (but written by somebody else, by a guy from Brooklyn) that it would never occur to anyone that I had written it.

Pinball deals with the theme of visibility and invisibility. But the key is not *Pinball*; it is *Reds*. As much as I enjoyed being a part of the making of *Reds*, the sad irony is that my ten-minute performance provided more social attention than twenty years of writing fiction. The tragedy is that with the bestsellers list— the ten or fifteen positions of importance—the publishing business went the way of Hollywood. Instead of attracting attention to what the novels are about, or praising the imaginative effort, we are being sent out on authors' tours to do the talk shows. Some of us, thank goodness, manage. Others do not.

I lived under the Communist system; nothing can be worse. I defend myself—I know my life as a novelist is at stake. So the publishing business became an extension of the media blitz and we become media figures.

I loved the experience of being in *Reds*, but I did not like myself in it. I guess this probably holds true for all of us who are not actors. The trademark of not being an actor is that when you see yourself acting you hate yourself. Actors apparently like themselves no matter what they look like. I turned the role down several times on the grounds that I did not have time. But the truth was I did not feel I should commit myself to something that was not mine. I would be part of somebody else's work. I would have to trust somebody else's vision. If I wanted to play in a movie I could have cast myself in my own movie—in *Being There*. I could have written a role for myself in the screenplay— who would dare to turn me down? I would say, "Either I play, or no movie." So they'd say, "OK, let us have a guy with a foreign accent."

I was afraid that, out of friendship, Warren Beatty, the director of *Reds*, would use my performance even though it might be a very inferior performance, and that somehow in an

otherwise good film there would be one pathetic moment. I
could already envisage not only my literary reviews, to which I
am accustomed, saying, "Why does he write? Maybe he should
do something else," but I could also see the terrible reviews
saying that in a great film the only unpleasant moment comes
with the miscasting of novelist Jerzy Kosinski, who should go
back to writing his gruesome novels.

Ironically I got fantastic reviews for my acting, terrible for
Pinball. I got the best reviews of any beginner in postwar history—not a single negative review. I knew right away that there
were only so many good reviews that one can get in a year and
these were going to be deducted from *Pinball.*

I usually get about half and half good and bad reviews. The
proportion has not changed with the years.

I do not believe in major advances in my imagination. I am
forty-nine years old. I have always been interested in the outcome of visibility and invisibility—all the more so now that I
know it firsthand. I enjoy anonymity enormously and I am very
good about it. When I want to be anonymous, I wear disguises
in which you would never know me. The sense of anonymity
was great because for once no one stopped me to talk about *Reds.*
No one said, "Hi, Mr. Kosinski, how was it? You were great in
Reds," so I would have to say, "If you thought I was great in
Reds, how about reading some of my books?"

I have no affinity for films. I waited nine years for *Being
There,* so obviously I was not rushing. I like to think that as a
novelist I have far greater creative freedom. Why should I surrender the result of this freedom, the novel, to a collective
medium which is going to dismember it and illustrate it with
living actors? Even with *Being There,* over which I had almost
complete control, a great number of people were probably disap-
pointed—they had seen their own Chauncey Gardiner and now
it is Peter Sellers. So in a way, fiction depends on being open-
ended.

When writing fiction, I have an idea, then I make a map—with very detailed topography—and then I write it, and then I rewrite a great number of drafts. I usually make it much larger and then I cut it down.

I had the idea for *Pinball* at least ten years before I wrote it. George Harrison came to visit me at a ski resort in Switzerland. I was convinced that when he came there would be a riot. It was Christmas time and tens of thousands of students from around the world were there.

When he called me from London and told me he was coming, I freaked out. I said to him, "What kind of a disguise are you going to wear?" And Harrison said, "Are you kidding? I don't need any disguise. I bet more people will recognize you because you live there than will recognize me." He arrived and exactly what he said would happen did. They played *Concert for Bangla-desh* in the local cinema and as if to test his theory, he insisted on going to see it. We waited in line outside and nobody recognized him. All kinds of guys came up and said, "Hi, Mr. Kosinski, how's it going?" Inside the cinema there was an attractive Italian girl behind us talking with some friends during the film who said, "Oh you know when George was in Rome I had a great fling with him." So I asked George about it. He looked back at the girl and said, "I wouldn't mind except I've never been in Rome."

The sex scenes in *Pinball* are very important. Sex was very important to my generation. I think to us it was more important than many other things because it was the only nonviolent force we saw in society, the only one that could create life, that brought people together, as opposed to ideologies that divided us. Sexuality was God-given, it was an instinct—we saw it as almost holy. I am still far more interested in people's sexual behavior than anything else about them because I can rely on it. I know it is authentic. That is why I visit all kinds of places. Someone asked me, "Why do you go to all the sex clubs?" I said,

"I also go to all the industrial shows." I went to see the new
dental equipment exhibit the other day. I am interested in people
and sex is part of that.

In athletics I have to compose myself as I compose a novel.
I am totally at peace with myself—both frenetic and at peace.
It is a great feeling. I feel very wholesome; I have no quarrel with
myself. In athletics you have to be spontaneous *and* controlled, as
in any creative effort. I become a work of art to myself, and I
like myself as a work of art.

1982

ON JOURNALISTS: COMBINING OBJECTIVE DATA WITH SUBJECTIVE ATTITUDES

The journalist's task—to report, describe, delineate, narrate and convey social facts—must by its nature result in a combination of objective data and subjective attitudes.

The transfer of concrete reality to this new dimension by the reporter involves a logic of its own and requires the selection and condensation of a large number of facts and opinions which the writer believes will best document his piece and best suit his adopted moral, ethical and political outlook. It might also be said that the writer extracts from the social facts only what he or she is capable of accommodating in his or her own creative outlook.

The reporter's purposeful detachment from the specific experience that he or she is about to convey is an indispensable prerequisite for the creative process. Inevitably the finished piece, in published form, will swoop back like a boomerang to that previous concrete life from which its writer had separated himself in order to describe it.

As soon as an editor receives the piece, he becomes the first of many readers of the work, and his emendations can produce yet further subjective judgment. "Once published," wrote Paul Valéry, "a text is like a mechanism which everyone can use according to his ways and means: there is no certainty of its maker using it better than anyone else. Furthermore, if the writer really knows what he wanted to do, this knowledge always disturbs his perception of what he has done."

Since our minds conceive of and empathize with created situations according to fixed patterns, certain fairly constant fictive realities—everything drawn from the depths of our memories, or dredged up from our subconscious, or wrought from our creative abilities—will distort the hard edge of solid fact. For we fit the facts of social experiences into molds which simplify, shape and give acceptable emotional clarity to them. The social event becomes *to a degree* a fiction—a structure made to accommodate the reporter's vision, his feelings and attitudes. If it were not for these structures, journalism would be too personal for the reporter to create, much less for the audience to grasp.

No reporting is the same as reality; rather, reporting is the using of symbols by which an otherwise unstatable subjective reality is made manifest. Even film, which is of all the arts the most capable of portraying the literal, is edited; if it were not, it would be either incomprehensible or indigestible to the audience.

The editing process occurs in all media: Describing is an automatic process of editing, just as editing is a form of writing. "Expression begins where thought ends," says Camus. That is what all creation, including reporting, is about. The journalist must edit out what is unimportant or noncommunicable in dramatic situations and paraphrase what is left. One could therefore say, "Reporting begins where emotion ends."

The journalist transmutes the experiences around us into little films. One example of the transformation of an experience into a fine piece of reporting is Albert Camus' "Return to Tipasa." Camus had once lived in Tipasa and was now revisiting it, but in his article he subordinated the details of his actual visit to those emotions the visit stirred in him and which he wished to convey.

Thus, even the best journalism, the most faithful reporting, is to a substantial degree an evocation of circumstances in which the literal and the symbolic approach each other so closely that *from the confrontation arises the meaning.*

1981

ARTISTS AND EYE

ON SCULPTURE:
SCULPTORIDS OF
RHONDA ROLAND
SHEARER

Radiating space and time, proximity and distance, like *Constellation Sculptoris*, Shearer's bronzes—call them sculptorids—share with other most ingenious creations the orbit of wonderment. Injecting life into lifeless metal and turning living matter into a spectacle of the most pliant metallic forms, her *Still Lives* and *Geometric Proportions in Nature*, bring to mind Umberto Boccioni's *Unique Forms of Continuity in Space*, the deftly condensed Alberto Giacometti's *Man* and *City Square* and the misleadingly small, but potent, hand-held bronzes of Henri Gaudier-Brzeska—be it his *Duck* or *Red Stone Dancer*. Shearer's sculptorids share the symbolic with *Pierced Form* by Barbara Hepworth, and Max Ernst's *The Table is Set*, and with many works of Isamu Noguchi and Man Ray.

In her manifold, multisurfaced metalwork, Shearer cultivates the inventive tradition of repoussé movements which flourished at the turn of the century at, among others, the Keswick School of Industrial Art in London and the Chicago Arts and Crafts Society. In 1896, the *Magazine of Arts* pronounced the metalwork of W.A.S. Benson as "palpitatingly modern"—a description which, given the craftsmanship alone, eminently fits Shearer's work. As classic in their vitality and force of expression as the anonymous Nuraghic bronze figurines of the second millennium B.C., which implanted the passion and fantasy of the Near East into realistically confrontational forms of Western art, Shearer's bronzes seem to have succeeded in casting the mystery of living form upon the symmetry imposed by perception—and not the other way around.

What she asks of herself, each of her sculptorids seems to be asking of us: her works (one of which is titled *Principia*) ask, How principal is form? What are principles of matter? Into whose mold does the bronze flow? Was it opened by nature itself—or by the nature of the vision of the sculptress? What are the crevices of human vision and of space which bronze itself cannot fill but which, alternating in depth like a circle on the Necker Cube, are filled by the wondrously creative specter of the eye—and the associations triggered by the work of art in the human spectator?

And, in the *Still Life* series, her sculptorids make us ponder where their stillness comes from? Is the geometry of her *Geometric Cactus* and *Geometric Tree* an aspect derived from the cactus and the tree or is it the artist's innermost property?

In *The Act of Creation* Arthur Koestler reminds us that painters, sculptors and architects often seek inspiration in science and scientific theories. Dürer and Leonardo sought it in the "ultimate law of proportion." Cézanne believed that "everything in nature is modeled on the sphere, the cone and the cylinder," while to Braque only the cube made sense. In Koestler's words, "the intellectual aspect of this eureka process is closely akin to the scientist's—or the mystic's—'spontaneous illumination.' "

Shearer's recent works, the *Ambiguous Figures*, refer us to a phenomenon known to science: namely, that the selfsame, unvaried stimulation of the human eye can lead to evoking images totally opposite to one another—as well as a twin, or quasi replica, of what was seen. "The most common ambiguous

figures are of two kinds: figures which alternate as 'object' or
'ground,' and those which spontaneously change their position in depth," writes Richard L. Gregory in his *Eye and Brain: The Psychology of Seeing.*

Shearer's sculptorids can best be interpreted using the Japanese notions of *ma* and *oku*, the quintessential principles which, in Japanese art, so forcefully mediate between what nature randomly makes and what the artist most artfully can make of it—for instance, turning living Japanese gardens into vital yet cubic enclosures. Derived from the Buddhist Great Void (Sun-yata)—a oneness of man and nature, and a realization of both through Buddha, and, in particular from the "form is emptiness, and emptiness is form" principle, conceptualized in India (circa 200 A.D.) by Nagarjuna, the Mahayana Buddhist, *ma* is a void activated by meaning. Adopted by Shinto, *ma* in sculpture corresponds to "in between"; to what in homogenous Japanese verbal communication (since the Japanese writing system is of an altogether different origin) is called *haragei*: a gap, or a pause. *Haragei* is an interval which, colored by what precedes it in the mind and what is anticipated by us to follow, is neither a sound nor silence.

To Michihiro Matsumoto, "*ma* is that moment unbridled by contradictions—[the] contrast between part and whole; it is the moment that allows one to be aware of and be part of his surroundings."* Other Japanese artists perceive *ma* as the interval between both connecting and separating two things or phenomena which, occurring continuously, glue, so to speak, our perception of space to that of time and of time to space. (Quite appropriately, some of Shearer's bronzes are titled *Space/Time Intervals.*

Writes Fumihiko Maki:

* Michihiro Matsumoto, Haragei. (*Tokyo Kodansha International*, 1984, p. 38)

The ambiguity of boundaries as layered "envelopes" (*ma*), is closely related to the ambiguity of a center (*oku*) . . . The *oku* is the original point (mental touchstone) in the minds of people who observe or create it, and hence becomes the invisible center; or more precisely, it is a convenience . . . which denies absolute objects or symbols such as the notion of center . . . for it does not need to be made explicit to others.[*]

Like Marcel Duchamp (as an example, see his *To Be Looked at [from the Other Side of the Glass] with One Eye, Close to, for Almost an Hour* oil paint, silver leaf, lead wire, and magnifying lens on glass (cracked), mounted between two panes of glass in a standing metal frame on a painted wood base), Shearer searches:

> . . . for the three-dimensional eye, [since] a sphere always remains the same whatever the point of view. But a sphere (for the four-dimensional perception displacing itself four-dimensionally until the four-dimensional "rays" become the visual rays of the ordinary three-dimensional eye) undergoes many changes in shape until the sphere in three dimensions gradually decreases in volume, without decreasing in radius, to simple plane circle. (Marcel Duchamp)[†]

For Shearer, wedged-in bronze, mirrored surfaces or mirrors provide her sculptorids with both a physical means of reflection and a metaphor for such a three-dimensional eye. This is her *ma* and *oku*, insinuated between the artist's eye and the world. This is the "in-between" dialectically connecting and separating abstract and concrete, constant and variable, chaos and order,

[*]Fumihiko Maki, "Japanese City Spaces and the Concept of Oku," *JA The Japan Architect*, May 1979, pp. 51–62

[†]From *Marcel Duchamp's Notes From The Large Glass: An N-Dimensional Analysis* by Craig E. Adcock. Ann Arbor, 1983, p. 92

spiritual and material—all the dualities so artfully conceptualized by Mondrian's "mutual relationships" one of the metaphysical influences Shearer absorbed, for instance, in *What Is Curve
and Right Angle(?)* and *Reggae*.

Like *Pangea*, Shearer's sculptorid installed in Manhattan at
the intersection of Twenty-third Street, Fifth Avenue and
Broadway, her *Ambiguous Bronzes* tempt us the way Myron's
Bronze Cow (fifth century B.C.) did—set in a public market
place, it tempted the living bulls. They could not pass by it
without making a pass at it.

1990

PHOTOGRAPHY AS ART

The purpose of the art of fiction is to trigger in the reader—
through an original, conscious choice of words (which are, by
their nature, always abstract)—a spontaneous evoking of people
and objects, acts and situations, that are concrete. The purpose
of the art of photography is to trigger in the spectator—through
an original conscious choice of graphic and photographic images
(that are, by their nature, always concrete)—a spontaneous
evoking of an interplay of composition, light, shade and space,
a new visual ordering abstract in its impact. Thus the essence
of both of these art forms depends on how profoundly each
one can affect us: literature in its movement from abstract to
concrete, photography from concrete to abstract.

1980

ON FILM AND
LITERATURE

Like painting and music, film and literature are two sovereign forms of art, each one commanding unique means of expression, each one demanding a particular involvement.

Film starts from *without*, with the concrete, the prerecorded moving images that depend on the spectator's willingness to become a witness to the drama portrayed on the screen. Literary experience starts from *within*, with the general, the language, and depends on reader's effort and ability to evoke concrete characters, situations, memories and feelings.

Thus, because a single picture is not a word, moving pictures not a page, and a film not a novel, I vote for the creative enforcement of Simon's Law governing the cinematic adaptations of novels: "If it is worth doing, it cannot be done; if it can be done, it was not worth it."

1977

THE
SPORTY
SELF

HOW I LEARNED
TO LEVITATE
IN WATER

At the age of ten, while ice-skating on a lake in Poland, I was pushed under the ice as a prank by village kids and, choking, barely made it to the surface. I knew water was not my element. Ever since—whether in an ocean, river, lake, swimming pool or, occasionally, even in a bathtub—I've been terrified of water closing over me again. It is because of this fear that although I enjoy swimming I became landlocked, with skiing and horseback riding as my favorite sports and exercise.

Last year, while vacationing in Bangkok, a Venice of the Orient, I became aware of the ease and freedom with which the Thais approach water—the smallest children and the oldest folks swim and frolic in rivers, lakes and canals as if they were man's natural environment. One day, at my hotel, I saw a middle-aged Thai lower himself into the deep end of the pool, but just when I expected him to start swimming, he brought his feet together, placed his hands along his thighs and with his head above the surface, began to float upright as if standing on a transparent shelf. Approaching the pool, I examined him closely: several feet of water separated him from the bottom, and there was no device to keep him afloat.

"Excuse me," I asked, perplexed. "Why don't you sink?"

"Why should I?" said the man. "I don't want to."

"Then why don't you swim?"

"I don't want to swim," said the man.

"What do you do to buoy yourself like that?" I asked.

"Can't you see?" said the man. "I do nothing."

"But what's the trick?" I asked, watching his every move.

"Being oneself. That's the trick," he said, shifting in the water. His thighs spread, his feet tucked under him, his hands clasping his shins, he became motionless again, gently bobbing with the movement of the water.

"Being oneself—that's all?"

"That's all," he agreed.

"But when I'm myself and do nothing, I drown," I objected.

"To drown is to do something," said the man. "Do nothing. Be yourself."

"Easily said! Is there a place where I could learn it?" I asked.

"There is," he replied, a bit impatient. "Water."

"But do you know someone who can teach me *how to?*"

"I do. You can teach yourself," said the man with emphasis, as he turned away.

In the weeks that followed I spent a great deal of time observing, analyzing and understanding myself in the water. First, I reversed what I had always done. Upon entering the pool, instead of instantly swimming, I let my body sink, then surface, then sink and surface again. Then, instead of counteracting sinking by taking a deep breath and increasing the period of expiration, I started to practice a slow, shallow breathing. That made me less prone to bob up and down but only as long as I breathed steadily and more evenly. Finally, I learned that to stay buoyant for as long as I wanted, I had to keep my shoulders pushed back, my muscles relaxed, and my chest and abdomen expanded. After many trials, I managed *to do nothing*: i.e., I became motionless, inhaling only the minimum air needed to breathe and keep me afloat; throughout, the level of water never rose above my chin.

Now, whether vertical or horizontal, I could remain buoyant for as long as I wanted, enjoying the sensation of free-fall without falling. With the fear of drowning gone, I discovered a new enjoyment of water. Buoying up became pleasure—and exercise.

In time, as I experimented and invented fresh, more challenging ways of remaining buoyant, the advantages of my newly found exercise were apparent. I became more supple, my lungs enlarged, the muscles of my abdomen developed and tightened. For years I had suffered from sudden lower back pain and assumed it was a professional malady of a middle-aged writer who's been obsessively bent over his typewriter—and a penalty for my equally obsessive skiing or bouts of polo. But after a few weeks of buoying, the stiffness, tension and back pain diminished and then, for the first time in three decades, were altogether gone. Buoying can also serve as an easy introduction to yoga and other total fitness exercises because of the posture and controlled breathing.

Meanwhile, my buoying in various pools produced varied reactions. To children of every nationality, it was pure magic, one step removed from being able to walk through—and eventually on— water. To grown-ups—particularly the Italians, Spaniards and Poles brought up in the tradition of maintaining dignity and *bella figura*, even under stress or during discomfort—it was a welcome break from having one's hair messed up by unruly water. Raised on Cartesian logic, the French quickly agreed that it is buoying with one's head above the water that separates man from fish. In tourist-infested, space-conscious Switzerland, where swimmers already crowd one another, countless human buoys can float without so much as making a wave! And the Teutonic spirit of my German onlookers warmed to the military exactness with which even in the deep I was able to stand at attention!

1984

CRANS-MONTANA—
THE OPEN RESORT

E ver since, at the age of twelve, I learned how to ski in Poland, in Karkonosze, skiing has remained one of my steady and demanding passions, so much so that between the ages of sixteen and twenty-three I worked intermittently as a ski instructor in Zakopane, in the Polish Tatra Mountains.

At the age of twenty-four I settled in the United States, and during the ensuing winters I skied in some forty-five major ski resorts in America and Western Europe, always seeking the ideal ski resort, the ideal slope—one that, like a perfect lover, would always tempt, always fulfill, always leave me eager to return. To find it, I passed through interludes of quickies— skiing in some forty of the best ski resorts in America and Western Europe . . . but, as passionate as once in a while I became about a resort's looks, slopes or ambiance, it had always been either too demanding or not demanding enough; too severe or too mild; too attired or too bare; and so, like an imperfect lover, it always left me cold après-ski.

One sunny day after skiing in Zermatt, Saas Fee, Thyon and Verbier, I crossed the valley to the nearby Crans-Montana, in the Swiss canton of Valais. It was an instant revelation: While so many ski resorts are tucked in, folded into, or hugged by a mountain which, closing over, seems to be ready to fall on them at any time, from its natural balcony high above the Rhone Valley, Crans-Montana looks at one of the most breathtaking open mountain panoramas in the world, from Matterhorn to Mont Blanc—as well as at one of the largest networks of open runs in the Alps; a moonscape of open skiing, all the way to the 11,000 feet on the glacier of Plaine-Morte, allows you to look from any place along its descent at spectacular vistas: the Simplon Range to the east, Mont Blanc to the west, with the Weisshorn, Zinal Rhothorn, the Matterhorn and Dent Blanche in between.

Unlike so many other Alpine runs, Plaine-Morte, in spite of its name—Dead Plain—does not impose itself on the skier, but lets the skier decide how difficult, how challenging, how fast, how steep his descent will be. On Plaine-Morte you can veer from side to side and plunge down slopes so steep that if you fell nothing would stop you for thousands of yards; or you can waltz your way over gently moguled stretches that, one after another, pass between smooth ridges, narrowing into almost flat passes, then open into broad, easy valleys, narrowing and opening again—and all the while you are descending you are looking at the face of mountains so high, so magnificent, so terrifying in their solemn rank that you feel both mighty enough to challenge them and insignificant enough to know no one could ever begin to match their sheer grandeur.

My love affair with Crans-Montana continued. In early 1977, Linda Cross, a beautiful American from—would you believe it!—Montana, U.S.A.—arrived to profile Crans-Montana and my love of it, for *Skiing* magazine. (See *Skiing* magazine, November 1977.) While every hot-blooded—and hotdogging—Swiss, French, Italian, German, Arab and American male fell in love with Linda, Linda—herself a super skier—calmly rated skiing in Crans-Montana as "the best open skiing anywhere."

Yet, like a lover, a ski resort cannot be judged by love alone.

What made Crans-Montana so unique is not only its panorama, its year-round sunshine which usually guarantees a firm snow base (this is, after all, wine country), not only its eighty miles of open ski slopes and some forty ski lifts—among them six cable car systems—not just the fantastic run from the glacier on Plaine-Morte all the way down a 6,000-foot vertical drop to the village, its riding stables and its two golf courses—the highest in Europe! and the setting of the European Masters Golf Championship—but its openness.

Like its slopes and vineyards, Crans-Montana is an open resort. Faithful to the ancient traditions of Valais, with Sion, the medieval city and the canton's capital, only minutes away, it is also eminently cosmopolitan—a small United Nations in the Alps. There is no pretense here, no artificially rustic camaraderie, and none of the claustrophobic chic. Because everything and everyone is open, life comes easy—as easy, some say, as in a true mountain village; as easy, others add, as in the mountain town. And so for over twenty years, Crans-Montana and I went *steady* . . . and I cannot think of a better lover.

1981

P ossibly because my family lived in a big city, the first horse I remember was not a live one but a statue on my father's desk. It was not quite a horse either, but a centaur. I was about three years old, and one day I picked it up and tried to make it run on the wall. But the centaur refused. It fell on the floor and shattered into pieces. When my father reprimanded me, I said, "But you told me a centaur is stronger than a man. Even a fly can walk on a wall. Why can't a centaur?"

I was six when World War II broke out. Poland was soon invaded by the Nazis, and my parents, anxious to save their only child from the horrors of urban warfare, decided to send me where they thought I would be safe—to some far-off village near the Soviet frontier. They gave most of their savings to a man they trusted and told him to find a simple foster family who would care for me until the war was over. My temporary guardian and I boarded one of the last trains bound for the eastern border. On our ride through Poland we saw the Polish army in a panic: men, horses, tanks, artillery, cars, all in great numbers, all in disarray. After a journey of four or five days, my guardian probably panicked too. In any event he reneged on his promise to find a foster home for me and instead abandoned me in a small village set in the Prypet Marshes of Polesie. There I was surrounded by strangers, crudely dressed peasants, whose dialect I did not understand, whose looks and manner I feared. They immediately assumed I was a bastard child someone had thrown out, but certainly no one they relished keeping. Thus, my own private war began.

The peasants were harsh. They made me work for my food, and because I was so young the only jobs they could trust me with were cleaning and helping out around their houses and eventually working in the pastures. There I had my first close contact with horses, and the first thing the peasants impressed on me was how valuable horses were. I would be punished, they told me, if anything happened to one of the horses left in my charge.

I was small and light for my age, utterly inexperienced as a farmhand, equally frightened of men and beasts and the dark. I cried easily and often. I wanted my parents to come and take me to the city. I was constantly in fear of physical punishment, and the peasants meted it out to me regularly and readily. I worked long hours and was constantly tired. My childhood was over. I was on my own. Soon I stopped thinking of my parents and concentrated all my thoughts on how to avoid being beaten and how to get more food and rest. My greatest fear always, I remember, was that I would fall asleep in the pasture someday and a horse would be stolen.

One of the peasants soon devised a way to prevent that from ever happening. To make certain that I wouldn't leave his horse for so much as a minute, he fastened me to it. He would set me on a blanket on the horse's back and tie my feet together under the animal's belly with a rope in such a way that I could not reach down and untie myself. All I could do was to guide the

horse with the reins and prompt it with a whip. Because I
could not dismount, the horse's fate and mine were therefore
inextricably joined—if the horse were stolen, or driven off an
embankment, or eaten, so presumably would I be.

The Germans periodically requisitioned all healthy farm animals, so most of the horses in the village were diseased, under-
nourished and weak. They could support only a light ballast, so
I came to be routinely used as a "horse sitter," roped to the
animals I was supposed to be in charge of. Was I in charge,
really? Or was the horse in charge of me? We were certainly
not a centaur, a perfect union of boy and horse, for neither of
us was in any way happy or comfortable at the thought of being
joined. Often the horse would rear in order to unseat me, or
would rub against trees in order to force me off, or would roll
over with me, or on me. First I had to learn how to guide it to
the pasture in the morning and back to the farm at night; then,
more slowly still, how to make it do what I wanted it to do, go
where I wanted it to go. I had to plan the day, making certain
the horse was neither hungry nor overtired when I brought it
back at night. If it was, I knew that the farmer would punish
me, and my aching legs told me that being tied to the animal all
day had surely been punishment enough.

    Passed around from farm to farm, I got to know all kinds of
horses. I realized that a horse that is hungry or overworked
becomes anxious and irritable and will try to rid itself of the
rider who stays mounted too long, the annoying human fly that
refuses to be brushed away with a flick of the tail. Eventually I
became a permanent fixture on the roads and fields and pastures
of the village. The children and some of the adults as well
discovered that while I was tied to a moving horse, I made an
excellent target for them to train their slingshots on. When I
was attacked in this way, it meant the world to me to be able to

THE SPORTY SELF

get the horse to run away from my tormentors. Even though I could not move on the horse, or escape from the horse, with the horse's help I could get away from the rain of stones, pine cones, or rotten apples and potatoes to the shelter of a deserted forest or a quiet pasture.

Yet because of my predicament, from the outset I did not think of a horse as an animal of liberation. I saw it rather as the source of my torment. Horses imprisoned me. And they also continued to frighten me, owing to a variety of associations they had in my mind with hostility and brutality.

In the villages meat was always scarce. Cattle, pigs, goats, rabbits, chickens—all were steadily requisitioned by the Germans or the partisans. When times got really bad, the villagers would kill a horse and eat it. If a horse was slated to be eaten, the villagers would not kill it while the animal was cold or standing; they made the horse die in a heated-up state, its muscles softened by exercise, its tissue permeated by lactic acid. Running a horse to death required a long time. I usually got the job of riding it around the farm or the paddock, back and forth or in circles, until it dropped. If the animal balked, the peasant would beat it until it obeyed. When at last the exhausted horse could not go another step, the farmer would kill it, and in order not to lose the meat's vital ingredients we would instantly begin the careful butchering process. To tell the truth, there were times when running a particularly stubborn horse—or one that had given me trouble in the past—to death gave me a certain sense of satisfaction and, even better, of mastery.

As the war came to a close, the German army began to retreat before the advancing Soviet army. The fleeing Germans were followed by their mercenaries, troops of Cossacks, Kalmuks, Tartars and Turkomans, all deserters from the Soviet army. These mercenaries, who always traveled on horseback, would sack villages before the Red Army could move in to claim them. They would swoop down on villages to loot, murder and rape.

Then they would torch barns and horses. They soon became famous for their ruthlessness and their riding skill.

In spite of my terror and loathing of these men, I realized that out of my experience with horses I was somewhat admiring of them, perhaps a bit similar to them. I was, or somehow saw myself, as a deserter from my family, and I also made my living on a horse. Hearing stories about the mercenaries, I began to imagine how powerful and swift a man could become on a horse. Even today, years later, I am sure that my real attraction to riding a horse stems from that dreadful day when I saw hordes of these mounted hirelings brutally pillaging the village I lived in. That day I actually witnessed the power a rider has who is able to use his mount as a force of attack, a conveyance of flight and a means to freedom.

After the war I returned to life in my native city, and my contact with horses became sporadic. In the winter, as a ski instructor in the Tatra Mountains, I occasionally participated in "skijoring"—that is, being pulled by a rope attached to a horse running at full gallop in a slalom over a sort of icy racetrack. If I never enjoyed skijoring to the fullest, it was probably because of the memories it evoked of being tied against my will to a different kind of horse, occasionally for the purpose of riding him to death.

Four years after coming to the United States, I married. My wife and I spent part of each winter in our house in Hobe Sound, near Palm Beach and Boca Raton. By coincidence one of our neighbors in Hobe Sound had once been the U.S. ambassador to the Soviet Union. He frequently engaged me in discussion about various aspects of life in the Soviet bloc, which I had only recently left, and soon we became quite friendly. One day he offered to take me to watch a polo game at the Royal Palm Beach Polo Club in Boca Raton, where some of his friends played.

I knew little about the sport, but I found it utterly captivating. After the game I was introduced to several of the players, among them Porfirio Rubirosa, the colorful Dominican playboy who had been married not only to the daughter of Trujillo but also later to Barbara Hutton, and who would become the Dominican ambassador to France. An enthusiastic horseman, Rubirosa asked me whether I had ever been a member of the famous Polish cavalry. Far from it, I told him; in fact, I had been a witness to the end of the cavalry era as marked by the famous attack of the Polish uhlans—the best riders in Europe—against German tanks. Noticing my interest in his formidable string of polo ponies, Rubirosa said, "But, of course, as a Pole, you must love horses." I said I wasn't sure I did. "How can you say you are not sure whether you love horses? How can a man not love horses?" "I guess it all depends on a man's past," I replied. "No," said Rubirosa. "It all depends on his horse." After that, Rubirosa ordered his grooms to saddle two ponies. When the horses were ready, he had me put on a pair of chaps and we mounted. The grooms handed us mallets. "Polo is the oldest ball game men have played," Rubirosa said. "And there's a good reason for it. In polo you forget everything else—but not the horse!"

Four years later I wrote *The Painted Bird*, my first novel. The unfreezing of memory I experienced in the United States through speaking a different language and living a wholly different sort of life had patently contributed to my becoming a fiction writer. In much the same way, through introducing me to polo, Rubirosa had contributed to my feeling a totally new relationship to a horse.

True, polo is a societal game, but you don't have to view it as such. During a match, for instance, you don't converse with others, and your relationship with other players at any given time is fleeting. You are constantly reminded of only one other presence, that of your horse, for it is your horse that in the end mediates your relationship with yourself, with the field, and with other players. I quite like to think of the horse in this way, as a mediator between myself and the world around me. And whether riding, jumping, or playing polo, I also like to think of it as a mediator between my present and my past. It is healthy, I am sure, to remember times when the horse I was on seemed to me an enemy, which could easily have killed or crippled me; or times when I literally had to ride it to death so villagers could eat it. Such memories make our relationship a deep one. Perhaps even as I experience the memories, after all these years, the horse and I are in the state of negotiating a nonaggression treaty. But however we may instinctually negotiate, the final truce between us has not been signed, perhaps never can be. Outside of polo, though, my whole relationship with horses is based on extracting as much as possible from the horse without imposing on him. When I jump, I know that it is the horse that jumps, and that I, the rider, must do as little as possible to obstruct his movement. I do, nevertheless, believe in making the horse aware that while I support his effort, I also have to guide him where I, his rider, want him to go: I must, in short, remind the horse that he is not alone any more than I am.

I vividly recall as a boy joining the villagers in dismembering dead horses. Therefore, I know the animal's skeleton and muscles very well. But I also know that the creature I ride today is not just skeleton and muscles; it is a complex psyche, to which I will never have complete access. I can only estimate it, respond intelligently to it, and pay respectful attention to it.

An example: A few weeks ago I was almost killed when the horse I was on suddenly reared up and caught me off guard. I was taking photographs and had handed my horse's reins to someone else to hold for a moment. In that instant I became aware that, in becoming too absorbed in taking pictures, I had, even if only for a moment, dismissed the presence of my horse and forgotten how vulnerable I am when I am on a horse. That domination over the animal that so many of us take for granted is, in fact, an illusion. We all know people—I am happy I am not one of them—who think of a horse rather as they think of a scooter. They would like to evaluate them both in horsepower, but that is a most misleading notion, for the horse has its own intelligence whereas the engine has only power. The two have nothing in common, really. Whenever I ride, the horse under me should serve as a reminder of my dependence on it, of my frailty, and of my slightly presumptuous intrusion on the natural world.

Mike Nichols, the movie director, is also a well-known horse breeder. Some of his horses come from Poland and have a long, impressive genealogical history. One day when I was visiting Mike, he must have noticed a slight ambivalence in me regarding his Polish prizes. "Don't you like them?" he asked.

"I respect them," I said. "It's the memory of how I first came to know them that I don't like."

1981

A PASSION FOR POLO

I once wrote a novel about Fabian, a polo knight-errant who also wrote books; I am a literary knight-errant who also errs at polo. Polo is a way of life I'd like to be able to follow, and so I would gladly change places with my fictional character. The lovely lady in the painting *St. George and the Dragon*, at the Church of San Zeno Maggiore in Verona, has eyes only for George (and Jerzy translates into English as George). She couldn't care less about the dragon, or even about George's resplendent horse. She sees in him a chevalier . . . and lifted sixteen hands above the ground, George's nose looks so much shorter—now, take a look at my nose! A touch of vanity, I suppose. You see, when playing polo I'm no longer a barbarian from Pannonia; I become a knight in full regalia.

If I could do it, I'd love to take a van-home and two polo ponies and, like Fabian in *Passion Play*, travel around the country playing polo. Too bad that my polo wouldn't pay my bills. Still, it's an attractive idea. Horses are part of nature, and taking care of them brings us closer to nature. When I see a horse in the middle of Manhattan, in this fortress of stone, I'm aware that the animal has been transplanted; but also that so have I— a part of me belongs on green pastures. I am sorry for the horse:

it's the natural affinity one émigré, one transplant from nature, feels for another.

My relationship with horses has always been a challenge of sorts, perhaps because my initial encounters with them were not very friendly. I was often thrown off. But some twenty years later I found a well-bred polo pony has as much in common with those wet horses of Polesie as a Palm Beach polo field has with the Prypet Marshes. By the time my first polo lesson was over, I had moved from past tense to future present, from rupture to rapture. Ever since, when I get to play polo, it's rapture all over again. No other sport gives me such a jolt of joy.

That's why I try to play polo every year and anywhere I can. By the time I arrive at Casa de Campo in the Dominican Republic where, thanks to my friends, I play most often, I am usually rather broken: broken spritually; my back is aching from sitting at my desk; I usually have the flu and a thousand things on my mind. But then I face the polo field, that spectacle of grass below and breeze above, and the instant I get on a horse—a *polo* horse—all the aches, all the pain, physical and spiritual, disappear. I'm ready to stick-and-ball for as long as my horse will take it. Within me a natural man has found a natural sport.

Polo is a game of inner contradictions and outer conflicts. It is a sport of the utmost complexity. The conflict of one player against another, of scoring and of competing, is for me the least important part of the game; nor do I care much about the proverbial supposed danger. While a trampled polo player flattened on the grass like a corpse brings back images of galloping Kalmuks—the deserters from the Soviet army—raiding the villages of my boyhood and the flattened bodies they left behind, I nonetheless believe that when properly approached polo is no more dangerous than downhill skiing, my other favorite sport. The danger in polo stems never from the game's rules and seldom from the horse; most often it stems from the player, from a misguided sense of competition. By nature, I'm not competitive—every competition is, to a degree, combat—and I experienced war rather directly. Enough is enough.

The nature of polo manifests itself best in the interaction of the player, the horse, the mallet and the ball. I don't care about goals, about scoring, about being rated. Whether stick-and-balling, playing one-on-one or in a game, the individual challenge, not the game's outcome, is the only experience that counts for me. This means being challenged by nature rather than by my fellow men. I'm convinced that, given its complexity, a polo shot is more difficult to execute well than any single action in any other sport. It was the richness of polo as a sport which made polo the king of sports, and a shot at polo the sport of kings.

Too bad I don't have horses of my own, or even a polo field; just my boots, my mallets, a whip or two and a helmet with a face guard to hide my nose from everybody. I depend entirely on the kindness of "kings"—on horses owned by friends and polo clubs, horses whose behavior I cannot count on ahead of time and who are not always regal or even very kind. This poses an additional challenge—but who cares as long as there is a mount, as long as one can enjoy being carried along on another being's back, impelled by a force flowing from another living creature. And what a magnificent generator of speed and energy a horse is! It is powerful enough to pull a carriage with six people in it; and I control all this power with my wrist. Combined with my own, this energy is channeled through my body, through my shoulder, through my mallet, all the way down to that fraction of an inch of space where the head of the mallet meets the ball—and then on to the action of the ball. All this speed, all this physical and mental energy exploding at the impact!

Still, polo is a team game. And as if one team weren't enough to keep me confused, there is the other team, whose purpose is not only to confuse me even more but to excite me to the point of being lost in the heat of the game. To be lost in childlike abandon is one thing; to wound others or to be wounded by them is quite another. So, no matter how intense my concentration, my awareness of myself presupposes being aware of the other players. When I'm about to make a back-shot, almost involuntarily I look back, not just to see where to send the ball but also to see where not to send it. Is there another player behind me? If there is I might make the shot only halfheartedly or not at all, since I easily envision my ball smashing into the face of the man or the horse. I won't forget "Pilo" Ezequiel Guerrico, a close friend who was hit in the face by a polo ball and almost lost his eye. Injury, pain, abuse and fear caused by the players spoil for me the polo ideal.

While my mind always plays perfect polo—the polo of Fabian from *Passion Play*, that master of the finely targeted polo shot—all I can do in actuality is to approximate that vision of an ideal shot. The mental game my body plays with my mind holds for me a never-ending fascination. No other physical act keeps me so engaged yet so detached, loose yet balanced, flexible yet erect. Hence, before making contact with the ball, no matter how quick the moment or how fast my pony, I can't help but remain intensely aware of each separate ingredient of the moment: the position of my feet in the stirrups; the pull and release of the curb and snaffle. I am aware of my shoulder, of my elbow, of my wrist and of my thumb. While the vision of the ideal polo shot remains fluid, my mind breaks it down into very small units. Units of feeling. Of drama. Of time, space and motion. Of physical detail. Of gestural action.

These are moments of exaggerated awareness, of complete absorption; they summon up all resources, mental, physical and spiritual. They generate a concentration so powerful that, for me, it comes close only to the concentration I experience when I write, rewrite or edit. But with a polo field for my writing page, these details also speed my action—and the action of my own polo story.

Keep your eye on the ball! The phrase betrays the desire to hold on to the ball at all times, at any speed and at any cost, if only with one's eye. They say, the hand will follow. The hand might—but what if nothing else does? Look at the ball! Full of energy borrowed from somebody else's topspin, it keeps on rolling through the grass, shedding the vestiges of the spin and the dew behind it. The ball and I. Now it's between the two of us.

I become aware of the dew on the grass; I'm sitting at the end of my mallet and then I'm in the ball. Not only am I looking down at the ball, but somehow I am in the ball, looking up at myself, at the same time. And as the ball, I say, "Give me a knock! I'm running away from you! You're dropping behind, I'm going too fast for you." And I am divided, both the subject and the object of the action. When I hit the ball I fly far away from myself, arcing up if it's a good shot; or I feel disgust if I'm being dribbled, hit and hit and hit again, right next to the horse's hoof. There is no sport as full of detailed action as polo is.

In my mind, the action becomes even more detailed, broken down into separate moments—as if they were the writer's paragraphs, sentences, words, punctuation. Turn the trunk. Shoulder to the ball. Get that elbow out of the way! Keep the pace. Don't race. Race kills pace. Free the hips. Calculate. Anticipate.

Ball control. The hitting ellipse—polo countdown—begins. Will you be ridden off or bumped before making contact with the ball? Will the transfer of power from the mallet to the ball take place ideally, slightly under the ball's equator, or will it be a mere topping? Here it comes! It's your line, the line is open. Go, man, go. Your mallet goes through the stroke. Press the thumb. Watch your wrist action. The horse is airborne. It's a liftoff—and just then the mass of the mallet meets the mass of the ball. Impact. Hit. Loft and length with a long follow-through—stay away from the horse's head.

A hit, then. But what kind of a hit? Watch that ball travel.

How many yards? Thirty, forty, fifty? Was it a real hit, a polo bestseller, so to speak, or only a so-so hack? Was it an ordinary near-side foreshot or a fancy neckshot? Was it a clever between-the-legs hit or a simple off-side backhander? And as far as your team is concerned, my friend, was it a bull's-eye or a bomb?

Who cares? It was polo. It was *fun*. Now you know why every moment of polo simultaneously contains absolute abandonment—without which I would never play a game as fast as polo—and absolute control: how else could you hit at a flat-out gallop a four-ounce ball with a wooden banana hanging some fifty inches from your hand, and shoot it flying at ninety miles per hour some hundred feet away without hitting a man or horse? The instant of connection: the supreme moment of passion and play, of spontaneous joy and premeditated mastery is, for me, the essence of polo, and the essence of my rapture.

1985

TALK OF NEW YORK

NEW YORK:
THE LITERARY
AUTOFOCUS

I recalled reading what Henry James said in *The American Scene*, when speaking about specific, almost anthropomorphic reputations of exotic cities of the world:

> There are great imposing ports—Glasgow and Liverpool and London—that have already their page blackened almost beyond redemption from any such light of the picturesque as can hope to irradiate fog and grime, and there are others, Marseilles and Constantinople say, or, for all I know to the contrary, New Orleans, that contrive to abound before everything else in color, and so to make a rich and instant and obvious show. But memory and the actual impression keep investing New York with . . . the projection of the individual character of the place, of the candor of its avidity and the freshness of its audacity. . . .

The reputation of New York planted in the mind of my generation meant, geographically, primarily Manhattan—but also Brooklyn, the Bronx, Staten Island, and Queens, its other diversely colorful boroughs. Above all, New York meant to us the one-and-only port of entry to The New Colossus as seen by Emma Lazarus, the American poet whose words are engraved

on the pedestal of the Statue of Liberty, holding in her hand
the Declaration of Independence.

A mighty woman with a torch whose flame
Is the imprisoned lightning, and her name
Mother of Exiles. From her beacon-hand
Glows world-wide welcome; . . . cries she
With silent lips, "Give me your tired, your poor,
Your huddled masses yearning to breathe free . . ."
(Emma Lazarus)

The Poles of my generation knew of New York's skyscrapers
scraping the sky, a city whose diversely creative roots and
branches grew out of the American Constitution and Bill of
Rights, Wall Street and the Garment District; of theaters and
cinemas of Broadway and the publishing and advertising indus-
tries, the city of the Public Library of Fifth Avenue and other
countless cultural outposts; New York as the unique human
amalgamate made of Yorkville, Chinatown, Little Italy, Harlem;
of the Spanish, Polish, Russian, German, Jewish, Swedish,
Brazilian and so many other national neighborhoods. Nevertheless, for me, as a student of humanities, New York's reputation
depended on what other humanists, other writers, whose words,
no less than those of Henry James, I considered influential in
casting the cast of my mind.

Their vision of New York would ultimately influence my
view of New York and of myself. In time, to a degree it affected
my art, just as, feasibly, work of other photographers, of Stieglitz
or Man Ray, for instance, could determine subject matter of
even most creative and innovating masters of photography.

Hence, among other reasons, I chose New York to become
my creative fortress. I chose it, as did for instance Thomas
Wolfe, an American novelist (1900–1938), who wrote *Look
Homeward, Angel, You Can't Go Home Again*, and *Of Time and*

the River—the very titles of which seemed to denote my own
predicament. Thomas Wolfe left Asheville, his American hometown in North Carolina, for New York in order:

> To love the earth you know, for greater knowing; to lose the
> life you have, for greater life; to leave the friends you loved, for
> greater loving; to find a land more kind than home, more large
> than earth . . .

And, in my days as a novelist, did I not, involuntarily perhaps,
follow in the footsteps of George, the protagonist of *You Can't
Go Home Again?* Wrote Wolfe:

> So he lived and wrote, and wrote and lived, and lived there
> by himself in Brooklyn. And when he had worked for hours at
> a stretch, forgetting food and sleep and everything, he would
> rise from his desk at last and stagger forth into the nighttime
> streets, reeling like a drunkard with his weariness. He would
> eat his supper at a restaurant, and then, because his mind was
> feverish and he knew he could not sleep, he would walk to
> Brooklyn Bridge and cross it to Manhattan, and ferret out the
> secret heart of darkness in all the city's ways, and then at
> dawn come back across the Bridge once more, and so to bed in
> Brooklyn.
> And in these nightly wanderings the old refusals dropped
> away, the old avowals stood. For then, somehow, it seemed to
> him that he who had been dead was risen, he who had been
> lost was found again. . . .

An even more convincing argument in favor of an artist's
freely pursuing happiness in New York—be it a novelist or a
photographer—came to us from Walt Whitman's *Leaves of
Grass,* an American monumental epic by America's greatest poet
which contains a great many evocative passages, one of them

called *Mannahatta*, (an Indian name of Manhattan) where Whitman wrote:

> *I was asking for something specific and perfect for my*
> *   city,*
> *Whereupon lo! upsprang the aboriginal name. . . .*
>
> *The down-town streets, the jobbers' houses of business,*
> *   the houses of business of the ship-merchants*
> *and money-brokers, the river-streets, . . .*
>
> *The mechanics of the city, the masters, well-form'd,*
> *   beautiful-faced, looking you straight in the eyes,*
>
> *Trottoirs throng'd, vehicles, Broadway, the women,*
> *   the shops and shows,*
> *A million people—manners free and superb—open voices—*
> *hospitality—the most courageous and friendly young men,*
> *City of hurried and sparkling waters! city of spires*
> *   and masts!*
> *City nested in bays! my city!*

Having lived in New York for over three decades, like many other self-employed artists I too sense from time to time a bit of the "haunting loneliness" which F. Scott Fitzgerald might have felt in New York, the very city where, seeking happiness, he and Zelda Sayre were married in St. Patrick's Cathedral, its mood evoking confessional, and honeymooned in the city's most proper Biltmore Hotel (apparently so improperly that they were asked to leave by the night concierge). We read in *The Great Gatsby*:

> I began to like New York, the racy, adventurous feel of it at
> night, and the satisfaction that the constant flicker of men and

women and machines gives to the restless eye. I liked to walk up Fifth Avenue and pick out romantic women from the crowd and imagine that in a few minutes I was going to enter into their lives, and no one would ever know or disapprove. Sometimes, in my mind I followed them to their apartments on the corners of hidden streets, and they turned and smiled back at me before they faded through a door into warm darkness. At the enchanted metropolitan twilight I felt a haunting loneliness sometimes, and felt it in others—poor young clerks who loitered in front of windows waiting until it was time for a solitary restaurant dinner—young clerks in the dusk, wasting the most poignant moments of night and life.

Pondering New York the city as the source of aesthetic *fata morgana*, but also as the boundless container of the realistic daily ordinariness, it might be of interest to view New York the way another image and form maker, the architect Le Corbusier, envisaged it in *When the Cathedrals Were White*:

New York is a vertical city, under the sign of the new times. It is a catastrophe with which a too hasty destiny has overwhelmed courageous and confident people, though a beautiful and worthy catastrophe. Nothing is lost. Faced with difficulties, New York falters. . . . New York has such courage and enthusiasm that everything can be begun again, sent back to the building yard and made into something! . . .

. . . I shall come back to America. America is a great country. Hopeless cities and cities of hope at the same time. What an idea of the action between these two poles is thus expressed, what a battlefield is spread out between these two feelings which exist in the gasping heart of every man of action, of every man who believes enough in something to dare to attempt it, and who risks catastrophe for having wished to bring back trophies to the altar.

For, beyond the narrow limits of the average in human things, when magnitude enters into an undertaking (Assyrians,

Hindus, Egyptians, Romans and Gothic builders), the result becomes a public and civic thing and, like grace, makes a horror sublime.

All the French people whom I met on the ship going to New York, all those on this ship taking us back to Paris, resolve the question thus: "Once you have opened the door on America you cannot close it again."

April 1991

The most evocative portrait of New York I know is by Albert Camus; it appeared in 1947 in *Formes et Couleurs*. Decades later it still captures the psychic essence of this city, a city like no other. Camus saw New York as the most private metropolis, a city where you are constantly reminded that it is the only place of deliverance where you and those whose company you choose for as long as you want can get lost forever at last. For me this is even more true now.

Thus, all institutions of isolation, of reclusion and of solitude are largely represented here. Although New York is one of the biggest seaports in the world, when you go from Manhattan to the airport it is not the ocean that you see—you pass along cemeteries which are among the largest in existence; a real sea of oblivion, these infinite acres of graves watch over the city from all sides like troops who patiently put siege to a city which will inevitably surrender.

But New York also possesses, per million inhabitants, more museums, public libraries, schools and universities, scientific research centers, places of prayer and lecture created by different religious groups, hospitals, asylums, old folks' homes, shelters for indigent and other similar hermetic places, than any other metropolis in the world. Simultaneously, the city supports the largest park—Central Park—in the middle of the most expensive real estate in the world, and a complete replica of a medieval monastery, the celebrated Cloisters, which depends on the Metropolitan Museum and was brought from Europe before World War II to overlook the immense Hudson River. You can find also a Swiss cable car which goes from the heart of Manhattan to Roosevelt Island that would be the pride of any alpine summit.

For me, an exile who left the collective umbrella of a totalitarian state, New York has been for twenty years a place of ideal solitude, a solitude which is not abandonment but shelter, the last stop before despair. All streets, all avenues, all express lanes and highways lead only to my own psychic home. Here in New York everybody nourishes himself by the reassuring knowledge of human relativity: for those who crawl on the sidewalks of life, those among us who are on our knees seem to be standing up; here innocence is the faculty to dissimulate, and most human qualities are merely well-governed defects. Here you do not change; instead you forget what you were before.

If it is true that when you are watched, everybody feels guilty; here in the city of solitude, where you are never watched, nor even looked at, everybody feels always innocent. Therefore, in this city of solitude, there are no disasters: here, each disaster is for somebody a long-awaited opportunity.

In spring, in summer, in fall, on the endless avenues and parks of New York, and in winter in its bars, in Manhattan, Brooklyn, the Bronx, Queens and Staten Island they are sitting every day for hours, the retired of the city of solitude, black, white, yellow-skinned; the old, the crippled, the deformed; the poor, the infirm; the mute, the insane, the deaf, the blind; the weak, the delinquent, the drug addicts, the incurable. It is here, on the street, in the bars, in the cafés, in the endless corridors of the subway, that you hear the multiple accents of

the voices of prophets of Europe, Asia, Latin America and the
Middle East. It is here in this solitude that the abandoned talk to the forgotten; the unloved to the failures of life. It is here where those who have lost all hope, hope they are mistaken.

Now you know why New York is my spiritual fatherland; here in the city of solitude, we—the refugees of the spirit—we get together to become vagabonds of our mutual utopias. And because here we are so many of our species, each finds his own kind. You see, in this city of solitude nobody feels the only solitary one, and thus nobody is really alone.

1979

As a novelist, I depend on collecting epic impressions the way others collect Impressionist paintings. Hence, ever so often, I am prompted to enrich my innermost Song of Roland—where else if not at the Cloisters, overly modestly described in its own guide as "a branch of the Metropolitan Museum of Art devoted to the art of the Middle Ages." Since 1938 (when, thanks to the generosity of John D. Rockefeller, Jr., the Cloisters first opened to the public), the museum has injected countless American and foreign visitors—men, women and children—with the quintessential cultural virus of the European Middle Ages, and has done it not at the feudal King Arthur's Round Table in Europe but here, at the Cloisters, this extraordinary American-made time machine.

The Cloisters menacingly commands from the high hilltop of Fort Tryon Park a view of the George Washington Bridge, the Hudson River Valley, and, across, the high cliffs of the Palisades, beyond which a large chunk of land was left purposefully untouched to keep the view virginal and unobstructed by modern structures—as would befit a medieval fortress.

Even though conceived and constructed in this century, the Cloisters is nevertheless prototypically medieval. It fuses, into a monastically cohesive whole, medieval arcades and other architecturally key fragments of five original cloisters brought from France: a twelfth-century monastery's chapter house; the Romanesque hall; a twelfth-century Spanish chapel; and many other authentic European medieval elements that have been reconstructed piece by piece.

Inside, the Cloisters houses several hundred medieval artworks: sculptures, metalwork, furniture, textiles, frescoes, ivories, tinted glass, illuminated manuscripts, painting, jewelry— and many more objects executed between the years 1000 and 1500 by the most representative and, in terms of workmanship, finest masters of medieval liturgical, as well as secular or personal, arts and crafts.

But that's not all. One of the marvels found at the Cloisters is a horticultural living collection of antique herbal gardens that, year after year, cultivate some two hundred species of plants known during the Middle Ages in Europe (some of which, I like to believe, are no longer found there)—a collection no garden during the Middle Ages could ever boast of! Another garden is exclusively devoted to plants depicted in *The Hunt of the Unicorn*, which is made up of *The Unicorn at the Fountain* and five other unicorn tapestries, which, handwoven in Brussels around 1500, form the museum's permanent collection and are among mankind's most precious treasures.

Add to all this medieval splendor a series of superbly entertaining lectures, programs, and special gallery workshops, which are carried out by recognized experts, and you will understand why I keep on coming back again and again to the Cloisters, to this magnificently remote medieval world—so remote yet so much a home of my own.

1990

M MANHATTAN

Manhattan used to be inspirational; it has become profiteering. It used to be freethinking; it has become freewheeling.

Look around: where the Diocese and Random House Publishers once held hands, Céline Boutique now joins Helmsley Palace Hotel. In this town, people used to talk spiritual shop; now all they talk is real estate and money. This is still a vibrant town—this time the vibes come from the pacemaker, not from the heart.

In search of inspiration, I moved to New Haven where I rented an apartment midway between the Yale Drama School and Sterling Library.

November 1981

The New York Public Library has been my choicest sanctuary, the quiet hours of concentration I often enjoy there shielding my haunted Self from my inner tumult, as much as from the outer.

Patience and *Fortitude*, two stony-faced lions guarding the library's most impressive entrance, remind me that long before I put my narrative head in the fictional lion's mouth, my Polish-Jewish family name was Lewinkopf, with (as I recall my father pointing out) *lew* standing for lion, the emblem of the tribe of Judah, and *kopf* for my supposedly lionhearted head.

October 12, 1989

GOTHAM BOOK MART

I visited, then revisited many times, the Gotham Book Mart in order to learn all I needed to know about the city also called Gotham. There, reading on the spot the books I had not known and could not afford to buy, I first faced my American Self.

A decade later, on a happy blind date at the Gotham Book Mart, my spiritual next-door neighbor, I introduced Gibby, a lovely young American book-loving acquaintance from San Francisco (who, even though heiress to a coffee fortune, worked at the Gotham part-time) to Wojtek, my book-and-movie-loving pal from Lodz, my hometown in Poland, himself a recent newcomer to the city of Gotham and the Gotham Book Mart.

And, happily, right there and then, Gibby and Wojtek fell

in love with each other, a love which lasted until one day in August, 1969, the two of them were murdered together by the loveless California gang.

Now you know why, each time I browse at the Gotham, I face a Self born out of adventure in the present and of past adventures.

1987

NEW YORK IS A CITY OF PORT AND SPORT

New York is a city of port and sport. Its style is both portly and sportly. A port in that it is a city that thinks of itself as being on the water. And at the same time, it is the city of the good sport, where you get along and don't complain.

You can see the combination of the portly and the sportly in the way some people dress with the club blazer over the worn-out pair of jeans and the smelly sneakers. Among the uptown Brahmins, you just see the blazers. Downtown, they wear nothing but the jeans. Somewhere in the middle you have people who wear both. That's what I like best and find most amusing. New York has never made up its mind whether it's a city for working or playing.

People here don't wear their money the way they do in Paris or Rome, or even in California. Style is an expression here, not a status.

1984

BEACH WEAR

When it comes to beach wear, we're not talking looks alone, but outlooks. To many Americans the tight and narrow bathing suits of European design appear obscene because, providing greater exposure to water and sun, they also overexpose man to his fellow men. To many Europeans the wide and long Bermuda shorts—they call them American coverups—appear obscene because, covering so little with so much, they invariably invite calls for full disclosure. So far, only the American and European nudist have resolved this dilemma.

April 8, 1985

Standing in our midst like people, dressed, dressed up, or undressed, most statues stand for more than they show.

Ever since I was a kid, I have been talking to statues person-to-statue, pretty much the way I talk to people person-to-person. Like people, some statues talk back to me, while others merely turn their back.

The day I landed in the United States I consider my second birthday and a prelude to my coming-of-spiritual-age. Soon after I got my first job—parking cars—I went to talk to the Statue of Liberty, the Colossus of the New World.

As Karl Rossmann, a poor boy of sixteen who had been packed off to America by his parents because a servant girl had seduced him and got herself a child by him, stood on the liner slowly entering the harbor of New York, a sudden burst of sunshine seemed to illumine the Statue of Liberty, so that he saw it in a new light, although he had sighted it long before. The arm with the sword rose up as if newly stretched aloft, and round the figure blew the free winds of heaven.—Kafka

Run the scene in the present tense.

Imposing, the Statue of Liberty greets me with a smile. I smile back. It's a lovely scene: the two of us—two exiles, she from France and I from Poland—facing each other on this warm, though rainy, day on Bedloe's Island (renamed the Island of Liberty).

"Welcome to the land of the free. What's your origin, if you don't mind my asking?" says the Statue.

"I was born a Jew and I come from Poland," I declare, no longer afraid I might be overheard by someone who's not Jewish, or someone who does not like the Poles.

"Good," says the Statue. "To be a Jew means to stand for *In the beginning was the Word*, and over the centuries Poland has greatly contributed to the very notion of democracy and freedom—witness the proliferation of Masonic lodges in Poland in the eighteenth century, at the time when the very idea of Liberty was born. Better yet, witness the presence of Casimir Pulaski, a Polish freedom fighter who rallied the Franco-American troops in their assault on Savannah, Georgia. What are your immediate plans?" she asks. "I'm speaking of family planning."

"I'm not a family man and I don't believe in planning," I admit openly. "Family means possessions, and possessions possess. Besides, most of my family perished during the war and in the Nazi Holocaust, thanks to various statutes written to the order of Herr Hitler, the toy soldier disguised as a statue, and Comrade Stalin, the caudillo pretending to be a simple comrade. This taught me a lesson in man's perishability. As a result, while I still belong to the family of man, and still keep on talking to various human and humane statues, I no longer intend to start my own family."

"I understand," says the Statue. "How about choosing a new profession?"

"As an exile, I'm a displaced person—which to me, a wandering Jew, means being mobile," I profess freely. "I don't ever again want to be a kept man—a man kept by his profession, or by the state or a company, or even by the company he keeps. Now I'm finally free to follow my own calling—a call I first learned from Jack London."

"Good!" The Statue nods her approval. "Since the gold-digging days of Jack London, many young Europeans have called upon our free-enterprise system—our call of the wild—in order to strike gold." Offhandedly she looks to her left, at Ellis Island, through which so many of them came. "When will you start digging?" she asks.

"I've already started," I say to her with the pride of a new entrepreneur.

"And what have you discovered?"

Who am I? A mere chip from the block of being? Am I not both the chisel and the marble? Being and foreseeing? Being and bringing into being?—Abraham J. Heschel

"I discovered myself," I say with the pride of an American self-made man (who to me is a man made of Self). "And I assure you that I intend to keep on digging."

Homo duplex has in my case more than one meaning.—Joseph Conrad

"Whose capital and what tools do you employ in your self-centered enterprise?" she wants to know.

"The Good Book, for capital, and writing in English, for my only tool," I say firmly. "You see, Miss Liberty, where I come from, the state's inspection left as little place for introspection, for speculating about oneself, as it did for a political suspect or speculation on the marketplace. One day I intend to become a full-fledged writer—just on spec," I say without hesitating. . . .

It is easier to sail many thousands of miles through cold and
storm and cannibals, in a government ship, with five hundred
men and boys to assist one, than it is to explore the private sea,
the Atlantic and Pacific Ocean of one's being alone.—Thoreau

1986

PEOPLE, PLACES AND ME

CHARISMA
CAMOUFLAGES
MORTALITY

The pope is the most visible, the best known, the most-easily identifiable vessel of religious worship we know. To countless millions around the world, the Pope is the Holy Father, the embodiment of the divine, a source of love and understanding, a mediator between earth and heaven, between the human and the superhuman, between the actual and the eternal.

In fact, his charisma, though conferred by men, is far beyond any mere gift of exalted visibility, which other men in office also enjoy. His charisma is so powerful that while it influences and attracts, it also camouflages the fact that the Pope is mortal, flesh and blood, as real a man as every other man, born of others, a product of concrete historical circumstances.

I have personally experienced this phenomenon. I met the Pope when, as Cardinal Karol Wojtyla of Cracow, he visited New York in the fall of 1976. He was little known in the States at that time; many Americans confused him with Cardinal Stefan Wyszynski, Poland's primate. I myself knew little about him, only that he was, like me, a writer—he wrote poems and plays, and was a skier.

The two of us also shared growing up in Poland, a country whose spirit has been directed for a thousand years by his

Church and whose people have in recent times suffered oppression at the totalitarian hands of Stalin's successors. Today, when my thoughts are in Rome with him, my emotions broken by the bullets that struck him, I find it difficult, almost impossible, to believe that some five years ago I walked calmly down New York streets with him. I remember how we stopped at a newsstand to glance through skiing magazines, reminisced about studying philosophy in Poland, and talked about Zakopane, a ski resort in his diocese that we both knew very well. When, that day, I said good-bye to this humble, articulate, simple, creative man I could scarcely imagine that he would soon be called Pope John Paul II.

If such a charismatic figure—whether he be Pope or President—steps too easily or too often into our midst—whether to bless us, or shake our hand—he unwittingly challenges his separation from ordinary people, the very principle of his own charisma. In so doing, he shatters in the eyes of some men— particularly the emotionally unstable ones—the very evidence of his greatness. Given an easy chance of proximity to the great man, the potential assassin seizes his or her opportunity to kill him as if, in a brief destructive moment, to usurp the very charisma the great man sacrificed, in their eyes, by stepping down to them, by attempting to prove he was, once again, ordinary.

1981

SOLZHENITSYN: THE DISENCHANTED PILGRIM

The United States draws so many Eastern European émigrés because it is still the land of freedom.

These newcomers are offspring of the Nazi or Soviet-inspired totalitarianism: a society in which a person is a mere tool of the party. Any attempt at personal, spiritual, political or professional self-definition, any quest for a job or career change without the official approval is a crime to be punished. In this country, the émigrés experience the shock of freedom. Here each is free to become what one wants to become, free to say what must be said, free to live where, how and with whom one wants to live.

After twenty years of my American existence, preceded by just about as many years of surviving under the Nazi–Soviet dictatorships, I still experience that shock every morning. Here I am, a mere speck of humanity—still free to live my day as I choose, free to take sole responsibility for the acts of my life. Such joy is second only to the joy of being alive—and yet I would rather die than once again live without such freedom.

I think most of Alexander Solzhenitsyn's criticism of this country is not justified.

For instance, in asking of our freedom of the press: "By what law has it been elected, and to whom is it responsible?"

Solzhenitsyn shows that he has not only failed to grasp the meaning of the First Amendment but also turned against the roots of the best in Russian liberal thought, the very tradition which has inspired the best in his own literary work.

In his Harvard University address, he seems to have forgotten a historic turning point in Russian political development: the third congress of the Zemstvo Constitutionalists in 1904, where Russia's most farsighted liberals resolved that "for the full development of the spiritual forces of the people, for a universal clarification of popular needs and for the unobstructed expression of public opinion, it is essential to provide freedom of conscience and religion, freedom of speech and press, and also freedom of assembly and association."

The United States—Solzhenitsyn's adopted home—has to a large degree realized this dream of freedom. Could his very speech have been heard without it?

1979

Am I, a child of European fascism, a survivor of Hitler's Holocaust, a student in Stalin's spiritual gulags, ready to reject the freedom I have enjoyed in this nation for twenty years because Solzhenitsyn tells us that here "the defense of individual rights has reached such extremes as to make society as a whole defenseless against certain individuals"? Am I, who have passed half of my life at the mercy of totalitarian authority, really to feel that my personal freedom in this country is now endangered because, as Solzhenitsyn regrets, "a statesman who wants to achieve something important or highly constructive has to move cautiously and even timidly"? Am I, who came of age in Eastern Europe in the period of inflicted morality, really to fear danger "to the human soul" from what Solzhenitsyn calls "today's mass living habits"? Am I not here the master of my soul?

Sharing with Solzhenitsyn a despair over the millions who perished in totalitarian hands (including all but three members of my once numerous family), I nevertheless believe that he has failed to comprehend that often democracy is at best a shifting state between the tyranny it overthrew and the tyranny it might become. Even though freedom, tolerance and other qualities might be termed democracy's adjusted faults, these are by far to be preferred to the rigid correctitude of totalitarianism. Like a writer's work, freedom exists only when it is constantly interpreted—even misinterpreted.

1978

Some years ago, when I first went to Spain, I fell in love with a woman I came to know first as Maja Dressed, then as Maja and the Hooded Man, and finally as Maja Naked. I fell in love with her because I sensed she was ready to express herself freely—if only within—and I (a writer already in love with free expression) sensed this in spite of the fact that I was allowed to see her only at the Prado and only in the presence of that Hooded Man (an old bore who needlessly censored her every word). As a past citizen of a totalitarian state and currently of these free United States, I found such censorship particularly intolerable.

When recently I went to Spain to star as Zinoviev in Warren Beatty's *Reds*, I was reassured by the Spain–U.S. Chamber of Commerce that this time I would be able to talk to Maja dressed, dressed up, or naked, anywhere I wished.

I rushed to the Prado, where I was told I could find Maja later in the day in a public theater performing in "The Garden of Earthly Delights," a musical fusing rock and flamenco, church and military music, staged in full view of the Royal Palace by one Hieronymous Bosch, the "master of the free flow of carnal imagination," as the play was advertised in Spain's free press—which, let it be said, is the world's freest.

I went there right away and saw her dance. She danced so expressively (she was at the same time dignified and abandoned, free and controlled) that like all the others in the audience—her audience was an all-Spanish mixture of workers and students, military men, university professors, parliamentarians, and artists—I could not tear myself away. Did I forget to say that, in the central panel of that play (also at the Prado), Maja and her youthful partner (a young man also from the European Community) danced in the bathing pool, next to that giant painted bird, and—you guessed it—danced naked?

Now you know why my latest visit to Spain turned out to be not a visit, but a visitation.

1986

A BRAVE MAN, THIS BEATTY. BRAVE AS JOHN REED...

The parts of *Reds* in which I was to appear were shot on locations in Spain. By the time I arrived in Madrid, Warren Beatty had been working on his film as director, producer, screenplay writer, and principal star for over two and one half years on locations in the United States, England and Finland, not counting the three or four preparatory years he had devoted to *Reds* before the film went into production.

After being measured, fitted, and clothed as Grigori Zinoviev, I joined several dozen extras selected to play Zinoviev's associates, party officials, and other Soviet bureaucrats. We all now waited for Warren to address us and tell us about our roles in his film. I was surprised by how Russian all the extras looked, and, for a moment, I marveled at the art of Paramount's casting. As we waited to be addressed by Warren, I discovered that my fellow extras spoke fluent Russian—juicy, first-rate, contemporary Russian I recalled from my university days in Moscow and Leningrad. We began to talk: I found out that the extras were Russian émigrés who came to Spain in the late seventies as husbands, wives, or relatives of those Spaniards who returned to Spain from their exile in the U.S.S.R., following the homecoming of Dolores Ibarruri, *La Passionaria*, the famous Spanish

Communist who had lived in Russia since the Spanish Civil
War.

In their Soviet past, these Russians had been minor bureaucrats employed in various state enterprises. Now, living in
Spain, many of them were unemployed or only partially employed and not in their own fields; most spoke little or no Spanish. They all welcomed the opportunity to play in *Reds*—and
to be handsomely paid, to occupy comfortable air-conditioned
trailers, and to eat food prepared by one of the better local
caterers. Educated in the Soviet Union, they knew enough of
John Reed but little of Zinoviev—denounced by Soviet propaganda as a traitor to the Soviet cause, justly executed by Stalin
in the purges of the thirties. As film extras, they were all
selected by Warren from the Polaroid snapshots each of them
had submitted to local theatrical agents following ads in Spanish
newspapers.

As we talked, Warren came to the room accompanied by a
Russian translator—also a Russian émigré. I was struck by how
much the strain of working on *Reds* had affected Warren: he
was drawn, puffy, overweight; his skin had lost its freshness.
In his John Reed costume of worn-out shirt and baggy woolen
pants—which apparently, in recent months, Beatty would seldom part with in his off-camera life—he now looked like the
real John Reed about to confront for the first time Grigori Zinoviev, the Soviet leader, and the Zinoviev committee.

Addressing us impromptu, Warren introduced himself and
his translator, then introduced me as the man to play Zinoviev.
"For the next few weeks," he said, "we will all work together
and our actions will center around Zinoviev." He paused to give
the translator a chance to catch up with him. "As Zinoviev's
associates," he went on, "I want you to become in the film as real
as you once were and still would have been had you remained in
the Soviet Union at your various Soviet jobs. . . ." He paused
again and the translator followed. At this moment, I noticed

that the translator had failed to translate part of Warren's remarks, saying instead, "I want you to be yourselves—as you are and have been." When he finished, Warren turned to him patiently, "That is not what I said." He spoke firmly. "I said I want them to be now, in the film what they *would have been* in their past life—not what they are now." The translator looked blank and so did I. Neither of us had suspected Warren Beatty knew Russian.

"Sorry, Warren," said the translator, "I just tried to catch up with you."

"But you obviously haven't," said Warren. "Why don't I try then to catch up with you?" He laughed, then faced us again— and began to speak in Russian.

"I will try to tell you what I think about the film and our roles in it and forgive me if my Russian will not be as good as it should be." His pronunciation was correct, his accent not too heavy, his syntax only slightly halting. "It's very important that you will not try to become actors in this film but rather speak, move, and behave as you did when you lived in the Soviet Union. As director, I will tell you whom I expect you to portray in the film, and then during each take you will demonstrate—act *out*, so to speak, rather than act—what it is like to be an important party functionary. If you have questions, I or Jerzy Kosinski will answer them for you in our own brand of American Russian. Any questions?"

A young Russian woman, who in the weeks to come would fall in love with Warren, raised her hand. "You speak Russian very well, Mr. Beatty. When and why did you learn it?"

"John Reed learned Russian," said Warren, "and he learned it well enough to converse. This is a movie about John Reed; and, because I play him, the least I could do in the last few years was to pick up some Russian too." For the rest of the session, he continued in Russian, making only the occasional mistake of addressing individual extras by the more familiar "you"—*ty*—instead of the less familiar "you"—*wy*. None of the extras seemed to mind his sudden familiarity, as I am sure they thought it was on purpose.

For the next several weeks, he continued to direct the Russian extras—collectively addressing them through a megaphone, or individually in private conversation—only in Russian.

Some time later we were on location in Guadix, a small town known for poverty and the gypsies who still inhabit cavelike underground homes. The film's battle scenes, as well as the confrontations between Zinoviev and Reed on Zinoviev's revolutionary train, were filmed there on the open plains some thirty miles away. The town's only hostel was transformed into storage for props and costumes, and its ground floor was used at the same time as a place where extras were registered, paid, and fed in a mass cafeteria. The only accommodation they could find for Warren and me was in a small two-bedroom wooden house on the outskirts, inhabited by the aged widow of a Falangist general. The house had been in disrepair for years; two of its six rooms were a storage of old furniture, used clothing, books, and other memorabilia.

There was no hot water and the cold water dribbled slowly. There was no refrigerator. The toilet would flush only once in a while and the bathtub refused to drain. The electric wiring allowed only a single forty-watt bulb in the ceiling of each room.

Each morning, in the makeshift kitchen, a friend of mine would cook breakfast for the three of us on the kitchen's portable two-ring burner, and to make toast she had to prop a slice of bread on a fork over the burner.

After we moved in, the telephone was installed, its cord coiling through the floors of the small corridor that connected Warren's bedroom and mine. Since Warren and I needed to work on the Zinoviev-Reed verbal exchanges, an electric typewriter was brought into the small living room furnished with a table, a few chairs, and decorated with a portrait of the Falangist general and numerous photos of Franco himself, and other members of the general's staff, all in their formal uniforms with medals and regal epaulets. Appropriately for us, working on a historical film, they easily could have been the staff of the Czar. Working among these relics, I felt like Zinoviev confronting John Reed, trying to involve him in the inevitable downfall of the old regime.

A retired veteran of the Civil War, so old he was barely able to walk, was hired to guard our house; and, armed with a shotgun, he went about it with a Falangist zeal. On the first day, he almost fired at the widow—the house's rightful owner, who came at twilight to make sure Warren and I were comfortable. During the night, in darkness, the guard sat in the corridor; and when once I sneaked out of my bedroom and, afraid to wake up Warren, tiptoed to the bathroom without turning the lights on, the guard lunged at me in the dark and, missing, crashed into an easy chair in his path, knocking over his rifle.

Near midnight, exhausted after a full day's work and an hour's drive from the shooting location, followed by a quick meal in the hostel's crowded cafeteria, Warren would work with me on the dialogue, coach me for my performance, and, in between, dash to his bedroom for yet another of the many telephone calls he would receive and make every night to the United States. Often, in the middle of the night, awakened by Warren's coughing—in Spain he suffered from a prolonged laryngitis—and the guard's frequent trips to the bathroom, I would hear Warren's voice as he spoke on the phone. At such moments, again I saw myself as Zinoviev sharing a house with John Reed, a romantic American who, instead of devoting himself to the revolution and propaganda, still sought consolation in his telephone calls to those he left behind in faraway America.

Seville's Alcazar was chosen as the setting for the Congress of the Peoples of the East. A podium was built in the center of the courtyard, and banners with portraits of Marx and revolutionary slogans printed in Cyrillic letters hung on all sides. As the Alcazar remained open to the public during the filming, large groups of tourists—many from abroad—passed through it during the shooting, ogling the hundreds of extras dressed in their exotic Eastern costumes.

Mingling with the crowds during one of the takes of Warren delivering John Reed's speech, I noticed a cluster of Soviet tourists, easily recognizable by their dress, manner and the red-star pins. They had just entered the courtyard of the Alcazar and were baffled by the setting, the giant portraits of Karl Marx as well as the Soviet 1920s posters, slogans and red flags.

"Spectacular, isn't it?" I said in Russian to one of the Soviets, a middle-aged man with a camera and a guidebook in his hand. He looked at me suspiciously, but in the worn-out black suit I wore as Zinoviev I, too, could have been a Soviet tourist.

"Well, yes," he agreed. "Tell me, what movie is this?"

"It's about John Reed," I said.

"John Reed—*the* John Reed, the one who wrote *Ten Days That Shook the World* and is buried in the Kremlin?"

"That's the one."

The Soviet tourist was pleasantly surprised. "Is this the movie about John Reed the Soviet director Bondartchuk was supposed to make for years?" he asked, suddenly encouraged by the thought.

"It isn't," I said. "It's an American film."

His hopes dispelled, the Soviet tourist looked at me incredulously. "An *American* film about John Reed? Are you sure it's not at least an American-Soviet coproduction?"

"I'm sure," I said. "I play Zinoviev in this film."

"Grigori Zinoviev?" The tourist was taken aback. He reflected, than became alarmed. "Who are you?" he asked, lowering his voice.

"I'm an American."

"But you speak Russian."

"There was a time when I wasn't American," I said. "That's when I learned Russian. Now as an actor, I have a chance to use it again."

"I understand the Americans have buried the memory of John Reed deeper than we have buried his remains," said the Soviet tourist. "Who's making this film?" he asked, still curious.

"Warren Beatty," I said, pointing to Warren on the podium. "He is the producer, director, screenplay writer—and he also plays John Reed."

The Soviet tourist shook his head. "Isn't unearthing John Reed in Reagan's America as tough . . ." he lowered his voice, "as it would be unearthing Zinoviev in Brezhnev's Russia?" I said nothing, and so he shook his head again. "A brave man, this Warren Beatty. A brave man," he repeated and then, leaving, as an afterthought, he looked back at me over his shoulder. "As brave as John Reed, maybe even braver," he said, then rejoined his group.

1982

EGYPT, POLO AND THE PERPLEXED I

For me, 1988 was a year of self-discovery.

In February, I visited, for the first time, the State of Israel (so much of which speaks directly to my Jewish soul). Then in April I returned for a brief visit to Poland, where I had not set foot since December 1957 when, at the age of twenty-four, I left my then one-and-only homeland for these Jeffersonian United States. As if all this was not enough, imagine my excitement in November 1988 when I was invited by the Alexandria Sporting Club to play polo in Egypt—a country I had always wanted to see.

In Egypt, my inner Sphinx promptly reminded me that once upon a time Jews formed the world's second-largest community here. No wonder they left their mark on such different enterprises as the building of the pyramids and defense of the borders of Egypt against the nasty Nubians. Having heard this, my inner Sesame flooded with the memories of *One Thousand and One Arabian Nights* and my narrative beam came to me both from *Aladdin's Lamp* and the Five Books of Moses. Finally, the auto-fictionist in me proudly recalled that my people were first called "People of the Book" by Mohammed, and that the Koran openly fuses into one *persona* such diverse historical personages as the sister of Moses and the mother of Jesus—an imaginative leap like no other.

I had also come to Egypt to pay my respects to Rabbi Moses ben Maimon (Maimonides), the medieval Jewish philosopher who lived and worked in Cairo. After all, where would I, the always perplexed man of letters, be today without having read his *Guide of the Perplexed* at least once a year?

Walking the streets of Alexandria—Egypt's second largest city, which bustles with commerce—my thoughts went back to Lodz, my hometown. It was in Lodz where, shortly before the outbreak of World War II, my scholarly-minded Uncle Stanislaw (who perished in Auschwitz with most of my family) first set my fantasy on fire by telling me about Hypatia, the world's most fascinating woman of letters. She lived in fifth-century Alexandria, and died there at the age of forty, murdered by an unruly mob. You see, before I was born, Uncle Stanislaw published *Hypatia and her Epoch* (1930), one of many works he wrote about Greek, Roman and Egyptian antiquity.

In Cairo, passing through the City of the Dead on the way to the polo field that happens to lie next door, I anxiously stopped at the Ben Ezra Synagogue—the oldest in the world, where, it is said, Moses is entombed. What would he have thought seeing me walking all over the place in my Egyptian cotton polo britches and my American cowboy polo boots! On another day, riding a most spirited Arabian horse into the dispirited Egyptian desert, I marveled at the splendor of the pyramids, and at their sheer size. It took Napoleon to figure out that with the cubic content of just one Great Pyramid one could fence France with a barrier one foot wide and ten feet high—an achievement not even his Napoleonic brain could conceive of.

On the last day of our trip (not last, but latest, I like to think), appropriately for a novelist, I saw a most fateful fata morgana: the smiling face of President Sadat. Dismounting promptly in a sign of most authentically felt admiration for what he had done for Egyptian-Jewish understanding, I bowed to him as respectfully as I could. I was about to ride away when I noticed, standing next to President Sadat, the larger-than-life image of Naguib Mahfouz, the Egyptian novelist who, decades before he won the Nobel Prize, won the minds of countless readers around the world with his *Children of Gebelawi*. It was a novel in which, by bringing at the same time and to one place in the imaginary Mukattam Desert, Adam, Moses, Jesus and Mohammed, Mahfouz performed the darnedest narrative feast yet. Enough said?

1989

L ike many other writers, I have been immensely impressed by the Koran—a truly imaginative work which, fusing history with fantasy, prose with poetry, complex oration with a simple story, goes further than just about any other work of inspired art in the realm of rhapsodic invention.

Recently, I reread the Koran, this time in connection with the ugly furor caused by *The Satanic Verses*, a novel by Salman Rushdie which has offended many Muslims as at one time my own novel, *The Painted Bird* (1965), seemed to have offended many of my fellow Poles.

We must, in fairness, consult the Koran for guidance as to what to make of such dream-expounding fiction as *The Satanic Verses*. Says the Koran:

"My councillors, pronounce to me upon dream, if you are expounders of dreams."

"A hotchpotch of nightmares," they said. "We know nothing of the interpretation of nightmares."

Then said the one who had been delivered, remembering after a line, "I will myself tell you its interpretation; so send me forth."

It is precisely because Salman Rushdie allows himself in an

openly fictional fashion the dreamlike expounding of his so openly nightmarish private vision, that no individual, not even an ayatollah, must be allowed to force upon all of Islam one interpretation of this so patently grotesque novel.

Today, those who arbitrarily take upon themselves the mission of calling for the murder of Salman Rushdie would do well to put *The Satanic Verses* on a fiction-only bookshelf where it belongs, and for inspiration turn to the one and only Koran, which states most clearly that anyone wishing to enter Paradise must unequivocally substitute forgiveness for revenge and keep one's rage in check with infinite patience, rectitude and fair play. It is with this in mind that I must respectfully ask Ayatollah Ruhollah Khomeini to declare his order to kill Salman Rushdie null and void.

1989

SELF VS. COLLECTIVE

GOG AND MAGOG: ON WATCHING TV

Gog and Magog triumph in the country where for over seven hours a day an anxiety-driven populace habitually channels its own rapidly shrinking attention span into spectacle-fed TV; where literacy evaporates from education as fast as life's meaning from a shopping mall and humanness from a medical ward; where infant mortality and crime set national records even in the nation's capital; where nature turned by indifferent men into a poisonous junkyard quite naturally pours poison into men; where oligopolies and bureaucracy obliterate industrial grass roots needed to rebuild entrepreneurial America . . .

1990

With the advent of television, for the first time in history, all aspects of animal and human life and death, of societal and individual behavior have been condensed on the average to a nineteen-inch diagonal screen and a thirty-minute time slot. Television, a unique medium, claiming to be neither a reality nor art, has become reality for many of us, particularly for our children who are growing up in front of it.

Imagine a child watching this little world within which presidents and commoners walk; mice and lions, kissing lovers and dying soldiers, skyscrapers and dog houses, flowers and detergents, all are reduced to the same size, mixed together, given the same rank, and set in the same screen to be looked at. The child watches this crowded world as he or she pleases, while eating, yawning, playing. What is the outlook of such a child? What does it expect of the world? What can it expect?

It expects all things to be as equal as on television: neither bad nor good, neither pleasant nor painful, neither real nor unreal, merely more or less interesting, merely in better or worse color. It is a world without rank. To such a child, the world is to be looked upon; it is there to entertain its viewer. If it doesn't, one alters it by switching the channel.

In the little world of television, all is solved within its magic thirty minutes. In spite of the commercials, the wounded hero either rises or quickly dies, lovers marry or divorce, villains kill or are killed, addicts are cured, justice usually wins, and war ends. All problems are solved again this week, as they were last, and will be next week. Life on TV must be visual. This means single-faceted, revealed in a simple speech and through the obvious gesture. No matter how deep the mystery, the TV camera penetrates it.

Parents leave their children in front of the TV as baby-sitter, because many feel it is infinitely safer to watch the Sesame world of television than to walk in the world outside of their home. But is it?

Unlike television, the child grows older. One day it walks out of the TV room. Against his expectations, he's finally put in a classroom full of other children. A child who has been trained to control the little world, by changing the channels when he didn't like it, and was accustomed to maintaining the same distance between himself and the world televised for his amusement, is naturally threatened by the presence of people he cannot control. Others push him around, make faces at him, encroach. There is nothing he can do to stop them. He begins to feel that this real world unjustly limits him; it offers no channels to turn to.

In this unpredictable world of real life, there are no neatly ordered thirty-minute private slots. Here, in life, the child brought up only as a viewer must feel persecuted. Ironically, our industrial state offers few things that can be resolved in thirty minutes. But the teenager keeps expecting it; when it is not, he grows impatient, then adamant, disillusioned, oscillating between the revolutionary scream, "Now," and a political cool "So what?" He is easily depressed and beaten down. In this world of hierarchy and brutish competition, he is challenged and outranked by others. Soon he believes he is defective; instead of coming of age, he's coming apart. This breeding of weak and vulnerable beings knows few exceptions. The kids of the upper classes counteract TV by being involved with real events—real horses, real forests, real mountains—all things they have seen, touched, experienced. They have been given an opportunity to exist outside the television room. However, many middle-class children, and almost all from poor families are at the mercy of five or six hours of television a day.

My own attitude toward television is neutral. The medium is here to stay. The danger is in the use we make of it. I'm involved with TV the way I am with the motorcar. The motorcar has been with us for over fifty years, but it is only recently that we learned its exhaust pollutes our very environment.

In today's atomized, disjointed technological society, with so little attention paid to the individual, man needs more than ever the inner strength to carry him through the daily pressures. This strength should come from early exposure to life at its most real—its sudden pleasures, joys and abandonment; but also its violence, its lack of justice, its pain, illness and death. There is subtlety to man's fate which lies beyond the thirteen channels.

1972

AGAINST BOOK
CENSORSHIP

I f properly learned, reading can prepare students to deal per-
ceptively with the complexities of society. But it cannot be
properly learned if self-appointed censors are permitted to force
the exclusion from the schools of any literary work which they
label as "objectionable." Such action, however lofty its stated
motives, undermines one of the basic reasons for teaching contemporary literature: to present the students with hypothetical
situations—emotional, moral, political, religious, sexual—
which they are likely to face once they leave the protective
structures of school, family or community, or which they may
be struggling to face already.

Zealots of the book-banning persuasion invariably confuse
the literary work with the instructional manual, ascribing the
same purpose to these two very different kinds of writing: to
control the reader's behavior. Thus they see the reader reduced
to a robot, destined to imitate the events portrayed in whatever
book he or she happens to be reading.

Furthermore, the typical anti-literary mind perceives the
student as an ideal, isolated being removed from the myriad
influences that mass media, violence, social unrest, and commercialism bring to bear in contemporary society. Yet students

today are anything but uncontaminated mentally. These forces reach them despite all attempts to sanitize the classroom (or the living room) and quarantine its occupants. Still, the zealot, locked in a past of fictitious purity, tends to see the student as inviolable, a perpetual child, and will stress his or her "immaturity," remaining oblivious to the student's need to understand the wider world and to grow socially and emotionally.

One source of this growth can be the confrontation between a student and a book. Exposure to various forms of fiction usually teaches students that they can (and *must* if they are to enjoy reading) re-create the text's situations within their own mind's eye. This ability to visualize, to know that one can shape and control images triggered by the printed word, is invaluable. Its presence or absence will color every aspect of an individual's life—as a member of the community, as a spouse or parent, as a participant in professional activities.

In this act of imaginative projection, readers remain aware that, however involved they may be in the act of reading, they nevertheless stand outside the depicted events. Such forced separation between reading and imagining can act as a catalyst for a formative realization: that the reader is a mediator, able to distinguish between false and true images, between appropriate and inappropriate responses. This goes beyond mental or aesthetic ability; it implies the power to judge, to see a novel's people and events in moral terms. And such judgment demands that the reader develop—or have already developed—a working ethical code. This is the irony of censorship, that it thwarts the very ethical development that its proponents see threatened by access to diverse literary works.

Of course, the actual process by which students come to terms with their complex role as reader is a highly personal, internal one that cannot be taught. But students can be led to read correctly, to appreciate unfamiliar literary terrain, and to choose books which will challenge their minds and continually demand new responses, new ethical judgments. As their reading skills develop, so too does their imagination—not to conjure up deviant spectacles and behaviors, but to project themselves into complexities of life which are yet beyond their present experiential perimeters.

Banning fiction of a certain type from the classroom is one of the surest ways to keep students from exercising and expanding their imaginations. Denied the opportunity to learn how to respond to all literature imaginatively—instead of simply accepting it—a student can lose the ability to handle real and potentially damaging events. The tragic outcome is that the myopia which characterizes the zealot's outlook may become reincarnated in the life of the student who is barred from a literary work because it contains an "objectionable passage."

Clearly, life in contemporary American society is not easy for most people, including the young. Suicide is the second most frequent cause of death among persons between the ages of fifteen and twenty-four. (The most frequent cause, accidental death, includes many drug-induced, de facto suicides.) A recent national survey of prosperous American business executives indicates that more than half of them feel too pressured to enjoy life; one third admit that the strain and tension of their jobs have hurt their health; over half say that their work is at best unrewarding; nearly half have changed or considered changing their professions; and about 70 percent admit they have been expected to compromise personal principles in order to conform to standards established by their superiors within the corporate structure.

One of the bulwarks against this increasing sense of personal frustration is a strengthening of the intellectual life. Yet Americans seem to be growing further and further away from such a life. And, what is worse, they are abandoning the very tools upon which this life is built—a major one of which is reading. One fifth of all Americans are known to be functionally illiterate. During the past few years the verbal aptitude of American high school graduates has consistently declined—hardly surprising since that same graduate has logged 18,000 hours of TV viewing, the equivalent of nine years of full-time employment. Only now are we recognizing the intellectual destruction that this unreflective pastime can produce.

As this trend toward depression, passivity, and isolation becomes increasingly irreversible, schools are among the few remaining institutions that can help tomorrow's adults become thinking individuals, able to judge and function in a world of pressures, conflicting values, and moral ambiguities. The classroom experience in general, and the reading experience in particular, are two of the few demanding mental activities left in modern society. And both must be allowed to flourish freely, without arbitrary restrictions on what is taught and what is read, if we are to keep at least some small part of the student population from becoming emotionally and intellectually crippled.

Of course, ours is a free society and zealots are at liberty to suppress what they consider wrong and alien, just as teachers are at liberty to defend their authority and knowledge in the selection of material to be read. Yet there is a difference: professional training and the rights vested in teachers by the community should confer a special authority. But at the hands of the small-minded traditionalists, teachers are often exposed to prejudice and attack. They are cast as scapegoats and forced to present time-consuming, humiliating defenses. They may be called upon to testify on behalf of a literary work they have selected for a course, or to justify such a choice as if *they* were the proponent of an outlandish vision of life, rather than being the victim of a handful of hysterical parents.

Since the specter of book censorship can emerge anywhere in America, a general play for counterattack must be drawn up. When the book banners gather together, the teacher—in addition to alerting the teachers' association, the school, the library, and (if he or she is involved as an individual) the Civil Liberties Union—should promptly notify the novel's author, publishers, and regional and local book distributors. Some or all of these parties will no doubt be interested in providing assistance by furnishing materials (reviews from mass media and religious publications, scholarly analyses, and other pertinent opinions) that can assist the teacher in making a stand.

Teachers constrained from discharging their responsibilities must notify the community at large, and the larger the better. This is a national as well as a local issue; the entire country should be kept aware of every student's right to have access to all forms of art. So the national media should be alerted, in addition to local TV and radio stations, magazines, and newspapers.

Embattled teachers might also consider occasional visits to local magazine and newspaper stands where they can find materials which make the "objectionable passages" in school texts seem ridiculous. The students whose protection is so earnestly invoked have free access to these sources. A cursory review of local theaters will turn up films which portray violence and human destruction on a much more impressive scale than the "objectionable" passages in some school readings. Many a local supermarket offers boudoir confessional accounts in publications of questionable character, lubriciously illustrated, and placed conveniently near the checkouts for casual perusal if not actual purchase.

It is argued that such materials, though available, do not have any official sanction, that the schools are the guardians of public morals and thus should be more selective about what is approved for student use. This opinion undermines the more vital function of education, which is to help students cope with life by exploring with them the realities and ambiguities expressed in recognized literary works. The school offers one of the few structured forums for analyzing such situations—an opportunity to critically evaluate the human condition within the guidelines of literary value and human interchange. If students are exposed to a situation which departs from their ethical sense, better that this occur within the school context than behind some magazine rack. But the question is not one of exposure—that will occur no matter how protective the local citizenry might be. The question is rather one of analysis and evaluation—a function which the school is established to provide.

Finally, local boards of education as well as other community organizations would do well to recognize the importance of teachers who make their students aware of personal and world events, particularly at a time of political polarization, economic turmoil, and general unpredictability. These teachers, who want to prepare their students for various contingencies, deserve considerable respect. They are often attacked as "experimentalists," but they play a vital role in ensuring that schools will produce responsible individuals, men and women without fear of the world around them.

1976

W hen I taught at Princeton one of my students brought me
a story he had written. "I'm sure you won't like it," he told me,
"because in your work people die."

I apologized for being a member of the nonrealistic school of
fiction, and said, "You know, the very first time I saw you I got
the strange feeling that you were going to die young."

My student was dumbfounded: "I'm only twenty-two. That's
a terrible thing to tell a man!" he said, with real tears in his
eyes.

". . . To tell a man? But I'm talking about *you*. Didn't you
say that *you'd* be going to Vietnam?"

"Yes," he answered.

In reality, of course, I had no such premonition of his death.
I had simply wanted to shock him, to get an intense personal
reaction out of him by making him aware of the one individual
experience he could not escape: his own death.

This student typified many I have encountered on American
campuses during the past few years. He was one of those in our
society I call "dead souls." At best, I find they share situations:
they sit and watch films or television or listen to music in a
group, thus isolated by a collective medium which permits each

of them to escape direct contact with the others. Deafening sound effectively rules out every interchange. No one ever questions the intruding voice, for unlike an individual character, the collective identity requires no explanation or justification: it is, and that is enough.

Today, the attempt to define "Who am I?" is often replaced in each of our minds by the question, "Who do they want me to be?" or "With whom ought I to be?" Thus the knowledge we form of ourselves is nothing but a collective image which, like ubiquitous television, engulfs us. One image is interchangeable with another. But what about the self? I am convinced, and I see it manifested in almost every phase of modern living, from the corporate to the Woodstock ends of the spectrum, from the hard-hat executive to the professional revolutionary, that we are a culture of the denial of the self.

In its increasing collectivization, modern society offers every conceivable escape from the realization of self. Participation in the collective rites, such as mass-spectator sports, rock and pop festivals, is a stage in the loss of self, which has assiduously been rubbed off from earliest childhood by the collective-conformist eraser.

What the collective offers is the hypnotic notion that just as others are, and always will be, so one is and will continue to be; that one cannot fail because only individuals, setting standards for themselves, fail. The collective, at worst, only underachieves. As if betraying a profound guilt, the collective jargon sometimes tries to rescue a single face from the blur of the crowd. The phrase "doing one's own thing" is really no more than a mockery uttered by people whose own thing is to be part of an amorphous supergang.

The entrapments of collectivism are overwhelming: TV and radio, which permeate our privacy and destroy the aloneness out of which it becomes possible to learn to build a self; drugs, which smash the mirror of personal identity; the virtual disappearance of creative self-employment, and of professions and opportunities which ask for the use of the self; the terrifying featurelessness of the modern physical environment; the debilitation of the arts; the great gray educational machine; the devaluing and disparaging of the imagination: the "own things" of the eroded self.

Some of us claim to have the courage to give our lives if the need arises. Few of us have the courage to face it as it comes to us day to day.

1970

THE BANNED BOOK AS PSYCHOLOGICAL DRUG —A PARODY?

From time to time, my novels, like those of other authors, are banned by local committees who believe that a particular work of literature will drug the moral health of their communities. Now I agree that a controversial book might, in some respects, be considered the equivalent of a potent drug. My first novel was described by one critic as "a powerful drug on the mind." Another reviewer described my last book in distinctly medical terms, claiming that "in driving the psyche to extremes in an effort to survive and prevail," the work produced "a kind of antitoxin."

The metaphor is intriguing. Perhaps committees bent on banning a novel should consider the book according to its risks and benefits, using the precise, dispassionate language of medical science. In fact, it might be useful if such books were viewed in the manner of the professional information drug companies provide for doctors and pharmacies about new prescription medicines.

As a public service to all potential censors, I offer the accompanying sample fact sheet, in the style of a typical drug review, so that those who are considering the effects of novels on their

communities might find it easier to act in the best interests of
decency and moral conduct.

DRUG TYPE
Narrative Compound

GENERIC NAME
"The Banned Book"

PROPRIETARY NAME
"The Banned Book" is marketed under various registered
trademarks such as *Ulysses* (James Joyce), *Catcher in the Rye*
(J. D. Salinger), *Slaughterhouse Five* (Kurt Vonnegut, Jr.), *Being
There* (Jerzy Kosinski), etc., etc. Such compounds are generally
intended by their originators to be antidotes to the popular
culture.

DOSAGE AND ADMINISTRATION
Dosage should be monitored according to the response of
the user. The suggested dosage ranges on a weekly basis from
approximately five pages to one full novel. Treatment should
begin with one to three pages daily, with subsequent increases
in dosage and frequency depending on the reaction of the user.

INDICATIONS
Like most narrative compounds in this class, "The Banned
Book" is believed to be effective in counteracting the deadening
effects of cultural passivity, mental miasma, and other fantasy-
depleting processes. As such, it is equivalent to multiple incidents of actual life experience. Improvement should occur
within a few weeks, but to prevent recurrence the treatment
should be continued indefinitely. If there is no response within
a month, or if symptoms recur, another narrative compound of

the same class should be promptly substituted. However, the limited usefulness of all such narrative compounds must be measured against possible risk factors (see CONTRAINDICATIONS).

CONTRAINDICATIONS
Listed in order of potency:
1. This narrative compound is contraindicated for those determined to retain their high ignorance/passivity quotient, their willful inability to concentrate, their moderate-to-severe need for effortless fun, and/or their acquired or natural hypersensitivity to reading, meaningful conversations, writing, etc.
2. As with any other narrative compound of this class, lower page-dosages of "The Banned Book" are recommended for the weak and for immature readers.
3. Hypertensive crises have resulted when "The Banned Book" has been used concomitantly with, or following, excessive submersion in the following: certain Hollywood-type movies, crime/detective magazines, pornography/confession/romance tabloids, and other known Mental Growth Inhibitors (MGIs).

ADVERSE REACTIONS
The following have been associated with "The Banned Book" at recommended dosage: mental and emotional agitation, vocabulary/syntax buildup, increased creative secretions, existential delirium, literary convulsions, romantic palpitation, philosophical spasms, metaphysical drowsiness (seldom accompanied by nausea), aesthetic seizure, verbal tremor, videophobia, etc.

PRECAUTIONS
Use with extreme caution in persons with known history of videocy brought on by Visual Media Abuse (VMA). This

compound undergoes a significant loss of potency when taken during dreary film projection and should therefore be readministered once the countervailing condition is eliminated.

OVERDOSE

(See WARNINGS)

Information concerning the effects of overdose with products in this class is extremely limited. Acute seizures of literary infatuation are occasionally reported, and can be counteracted with any recognized form of sedation (passivity-inducing family TV shows, violence-inducing evening TV series). Experience with the more recent Bestseller-Television Adaptation (BTA) as a potential cathartic is inadequate to permit recommendation at this point.

WITHDRAWAL SYMPTOMS

Abrupt cessation of these compounds, especially after prolonged use, may produce syndromes of empty-headedness, blurred vision (seldom), depression of the central self, isolated bouts of videocy, and prolonged sore-life pain. These syndromes occur in varying degrees of severity and are generally the result of psychological dependence rather than physical addiction.

USAGE IN PREGNANCY

Used judiciously, "The Banned Book," like all narrative compounds, acts as an effective emotional reinforcement agent and increases existence-related tolerance. Hence, reading of "The Banned Book" by women who are or may become pregnant is not contraindicated. Administration of narrative compounds of this class is known to have been continued without ill effect throughout the pregnancy and after delivery; in some instances, the compound has also shown evidence of fostering the healthy development of the offspring.

WARNINGS

As with any other narrative compound, the possibility of abuse and dependence should be kept in mind when evaluating the desirability of including "The Banned Book" as part of an ignorance/passivity reduction program. Abuse of narrative compounds of this class may be associated with severe cases of self-awareness, as well as with the intense psychological need for imagination stimulus and for self-reliance activities. (There are reports of users who have increased the reading of "The Banned Book" to many times the recommended levels, achieving chronic mental agitation, as well as passing through sporadic incidents of self-examination.) Manifestations of chronic intoxication with narrative compounds of this class include severe reevaluation of user's ability to determine his or her own destiny, marked curiosity about oneself and others, creative restlessness, and occasionally, self-induced personality-libido changes. The most severe manifestation of the reader's intoxication by "The Banned Book" is literary infatuation, often indistinguishable from episodes of the creative act. As "The Banned Book" may suddenly increase the perception required for the performance of hazardous tasks (such as those commonly associated with the human condition), potential readers should be cautioned accordingly.

HOW SUPPLIED

This compound is available in hard and soft containers of varying sizes and quantities.

1977

JEWISH
PRESENCE

NO RELIGION IS
AN ISLAND

Abraham Joshua Heschel and Interreligious Dialogue

braham Joshua Heschel's theology of the Self starts with a startling premise: "Human existence cannot derive its ultimate meaning from society, because society itself is in need of meaning. It is as legitimate to ask: Is mankind needed? as it is to ask: Am I needed?" This becomes instantly liberating for anyone, particularly those who, of any faith but no longer with faith of their own, have been brought up by a totalitarian society or in an authoritarian state of mind. But then, in an age ridden with collectivity anxious to get rid of the individuality of any individual regardless of his or her age, Heschel went on to postulate what our society dismisses most.

> Beyond all agony and anxiety lies the most important ingredient of self-reflection: the preciousness of my own existence. To my heart my existence is unique, unprecedented, priceless, exceedingly precious, and I resist the thought of gambling away its meaning.*

*Abraham Joshua Heschel, *Who Is Man?* Stanford: Stanford University Press, 1968.

The key to such conviction is, as he stated elsewhere, the knowledge ". . . that every deed counts, that every word is power. . . . Above all, remember that you must build your life as if it were a work of art."*

No wonder that such a point of departure has provided a natural antidote to broken human spirit, as exemplified by the members of the generations surviving the German-Austrian Nazi occupation of Poland, where, in a mere five years of World War II, two hundred twenty of each thousand people of every age and origin were individually and collectively put to death or crippled for life in the most massive, most systematically executed genocide in recorded history.

This, already in 1949, in appraising eight centuries of Eastern European Jewry—the single largest Jewish community which lived there for the longest time since biblical times—led the Polish-born Heschel (who, in his late teens, was ordained as a rabbi in Warsaw) to the conclusion ". . . that in this period our people attained the highest degree of inwardness. I feel justified in saying that it was the golden period in Jewish history, in the history of the Jewish soul."†

Such tribute pronounced so soon after the Holocaust, by one of the foremost thinkers of modern Judaism, helped to unyoke an Eastern European Jewish "way of life second to none in its ethical and moral standards" (Max Weinreich, 1946) and with it, the Jewish identity (which for centuries fertilized the working of the human mind) from the spiritually traumatizing yoke of the Auschwitz-Birkenau Jewish I.D. card—the German-Austrian Nazi symbol of turning Jews and Judaica into fertilizer.

*"A Conversation with Abraham Joshua Heschel," NBC Interview with Carl Stern, 1972.

†Abraham Joshua Heschel, *The Earth Is the Lord's*, New York: Henry Schuman, 1950.

There are two ways of facing and inspecting human being: from within or from without . . . I suggest that although it is possible and legitimate to ponder being in general or the being of all beings, it is futile and impossible to ponder human being in general—the being of the human species—since my understanding of, and my relation to, my own being always intrudes into any reflection about the being of the human species. There is only one way of comprehending man's being-there, and that is by way of inspecting my own being.

Having thus fueled the artful veneration of one's life as the greatest gift (regardless whom one believes to be this gift's giver) leads in Heschel's words to facing oneself ". . . intimately, immediately . . . as unique, as exceedingly precious, not to be exchanged for anything else. I would not like my existence to be a total waste, an utter absurdity."

Later in his life, witnessing how in minds and lives of American Jewry the shadow of the Holocaust began to obscure (no doubt to the delight of the anti-Jewish obscurantists) the pyramids of the immemorial Jewish cultural achievements, Heschel foresaw the forthcoming of the "second Holocaust," as he termed it.* "Hitler destroyed our people," he said. "Now we let their spirit die." After his life, this monumentalization of the Holocaust diminished, at least in the popular mind, the memory and knowledge of cultural contributions made to civilization by both the Jewish Diaspora and the State of Israel.

Heschel's reanimation of the self, the human being's link to being human, proved decisive in offering to, among others, the Holocaust's survivors, life lived according to his notion of "the quiet eminence of one's being." Due to it, many of them, eminent or not, now live as victors over the Holocaust—victors and

*See Richard L. Rubenstein, "Second Holocaust" in *Power Struggle,* New York: Charles Scribners, 1974, p. 128.

not victims. They (and I among them) owe this moral victory to Abraham Joshua Heschel. Our disinheriting the Nazis of their claim of poisoning forever the living well of Jewish heritage with the ashes of the Final Solution was our final spiritual triumph— over such a second Holocaust—and a triumph like no other.

April 26, 1991

GOD & . . .

Until the age of six, I recall only physical—at best situational—events all stemming from my relationships with my parents or other children. Also, only behavioral not spiritual guidelines: how to be kind, how to recite poems, how to share my toys with other children, that's all. The actual confrontation with the notion of the Self—of who am I—other than as a physical being—came about during the 1939–1945 war.

At that time, away from my parents, I stayed with various peasant families—all of them Catholic; also, I had gone with all their children through the parish religious schooling in preparation for my First Communion. And so, the first religious truths came to me directly and indirectly from the Catholic Church. And even though I assumed that all this made me a Catholic, one particular dimension set me apart from other boys: I was the only one among them who was circumcised—and I was told that this made me a Jew. I assumed that the circumcision was a proof of commitment for which I could not be directly responsible, since I did not circumcise myself. Nor could I answer to myself—and I prayed to God nobody would ask— when or why or by whom was I circumcised. All I knew was that during the war with the Nazis and the anti-Semites who were hunting the few remaining Jews, my circumcision set me apart—and could lead to my death. Thus, throughout the war, my Jewishness remained a mystery I tried to but could not resolve. In a curious and ironic way, it was only my physical circumcision that, isolated as I was at the time, led me to assume I was a Jew. And beyond circumcision I had no idea what being Jewish meant. Going to confession, I never confessed to being circumcised or Jewish, since I assumed my being Jewish was obviously no secret to God, who might even have been responsible for it in some way. Also I was afraid that as a mortal, if tortured by the Nazis, my father confessor might involuntarily reveal my identity. In sum, throughout the war my Jewishness was never discussed: I saw myself as a circumcised Catholic. After the war, in the orphanage, when asked what was my religion, I wrote (I could not speak): I am a circumcised Catholic. After I was reunited with my parents, I returned to the Judaic tradition. In time, my father told me that, as a Jew, I must answer the questions: *Who am I? Where did I come from?* and *Where am I going?* And he left it at that. To answer these questions I began to study the Judaic faith. And this was, very briefly, my early religious profile.

I had always assumed that any attempt at my contact with God would be not only presumptuous, but actually contradictory: since, obviously, if I am his creation, then I experience God through the gift of life, and my obligation is to take care of the gift. The giver, presumably, delivered the gift, or sent the gift, or I inherited the gift from him. Present in the gift, the giver remains nevertheless outside of it, beyond my comprehension. To separate the giver from the gift is, perhaps, to diminish the gift. It is this miracle of life and the supreme mystery of being that unites me with my fellow beings; any speculation about the miracle and mystery of the Supreme Being tends to separate me from them. That is how I have looked at it as a boy, and, frankly, I still look at it that way.

Since meeting the creator through the act of my existence,

I'm more than conscious of the spiritual aspects of the act of life and the act of my faith in it. . . .

"I'm fearfully and wonderfully made" says the Psalmist (139.14). That's the most appropriate and proper dimension, since my faith in the spiritual purpose of existence presupposes *a priori* and *a posteriori* my meeting with the forces of creation; the only meeting of which I think myself capable, of which I was created to be capable.

Any manifestation of life and of faith is sacred; I would never dispute what they think about themselves, about their relationship with society, and about God. While I accept that others meet life and God on different levels, I remain responsible for *one* particular life—mine—which was delivered to me (I might respectfully point out) individually. That's why I have to tend to it individually, by myself, alone, in the privacy of my inner sanctum, and accord life *around me* the same respect which I pay to life *within me*. For me, any comment upon anyone else's religious beliefs is spiritually inappropriate. I'm a missionary to only *one* particular life: the life within me; and I proselytize only one faith: my faith in the sanctity of life. I refuse to pass judgments on the religious beliefs of others.

My prayer is my exaltation in life's moment; it comes to me moment by moment, always concurrent with the act of life, and it's the sole way in which I acknowledge what's spiritual in my existence. I consciously narrow my life to the acts of my faith in it—acts which are spiritually significant—and I keep setting aside anything which is insignificant, which obstructs my awe of creation. This is my prayer; other prayers are creations of others and I look at them the way I look at religions, books, poems, works of art—they are all manifestations of spiritual life. In my life and *for* my life, I have chosen one particular form of spiritual worship, and I manifest it as I go along.

I commence my day by facing the one who is facing me: my

Self. That confrontation is an act of faith: a prayer of acknowledgment, of gratitude, of exaltation. It is also a moment of awareness that life is not permanent; its gift is a spiritual lease, which might be terminated at any time.

I am, above all, a spiritual being: as long as I'm spiritually alive I can't be stuck. The intellectual, social, sexual, physical concerns are secondary, particularly when, through vanity, competition, false notions of achievement, etc., they obstruct the spiritual in me. When they do, they are sins.

I think of such fears and wants as obstructions of life—of deprecating the worth of me as a man. To counteract them, I remain grateful for what I have—my life and my awareness of its spectacle—rather than fearful of what might happen, regretful of what I don't have or what pains me. Perception of pain has always contributed to my awareness of myself. Sin is allowing pain—any pain—to damage the sanctity of life, to regress the drama of my spiritual redemption.

If I see that there is something that is threatening my happiness or existence, if it's a threat from within—if it's a threat by vanity for instance, or hurt ego—I confess to the sin of it. Then I analyze it, and I try to ban it, since, clearly, it clouds life, and, filtering the experience and awareness, it diminishes the joy of being alive. If, on the other hand, the threat comes from society—from, say, society's view of me or of my work— I try to disregard it, since I am not responsible for society. It's merely *being there*. If it's a specific physical threat—violence, for instance—I try to save my life, but never by combat. Rather, by hands off—though no hand up; to me, life is shelter, not combat; to me, the spiritual is already vested in the gift of life. For me to pursue the giver is to detract from the gift itself. The gift of life was left at the doorstep of my being, and the giver left it *without* leaving a calling card, that is without making the visit manifest. Entrusted with the gift of spiritual creation, I must remain faithful to it and enhance it by my conduct for as long as it remains in my hands. For me, any attempt at "chasing" the giver, is *ipso facto* turning away from the gift.

To me, the giver is implicit in the gift. Life is a very unusual household, it incorporates in it the notion of the creation. To go beyond the gift is to detract from it—to run away from it. Because I would dare to assume that as a mere human being I have a right to question the nature of the giver; to go beyond the spiritual vested at the creation in the gift of life, the greatest gift there is.

Death is the withdrawal of that gift. For me to speculate what takes place when life ends is, again, to go beyond the gift, to detract from the greatness and the sanctity of the gift—and of the giver.

Almost everything I have said so far I have felt after the war—both as a Jew and as a circumcised Catholic, so to speak. This was my spiritual inheritance, for which, perhaps, the Catholic Church was a great deal responsible since the issue of the gift of life, and of sin against it, came again and again in my confessions. In a way, all my novels are confessional, confessing to the reader the sins of the protagonist—and *maybe* of the author. They are also nonjudgmental: morally open-ended, they encourage the reader to judge what, to him or her, is right or wrong. My attitude toward life carried me spiritually undamaged through the years I lived in Poland under the Communist system. Because of how I felt about life, the Party couldn't do anything which could wreck me morally. *They* could never enter the kingdom of heaven within me—"the kingdom of heaven" is the gift of life. Ever since I emerged from the "kindergarten" of World War II, I've refused to commit my spiritual being to anything but life itself. I will not commit it to bureaucracy; I will not commit it to political power; I will not commit it to any institution, association, or group which combats life or tries to institutionally modify the beliefs and attitudes of others, or passing socially binding judgments. Hence, for me, the calling of a novelist is an appropriate one; fiction is a suspension of disbelief—not a statement of belief; and since it deals in imaginary situations, it cannot slander or damage or seduce or convert anyone; it is in no way a "how-to." It tells a tale but it says nothing. As a novelist, I'm the furthest removed from being a missionary to any particular faith and to any particular church.

Maybe it was the Holocaust which turned me toward life and exaltation in its gift; during the war I saw life destroyed— brutally taken away. I saw the frailty of man, both physical and spiritual. I recognized once and for all that if a human being— a creature so small, so frail, so short-lasting—is endowed with life, with such a generous gift, and still thinks it's not enough and wants to know what happens in the afterlife—well, that's a sin. What I have said is not based on any system of belief. It is merely what I feel when I confront myself on waking up. It is my private faith. In fact, I feel a bit guilty about sharing it with you since I haven't really done it directly—only indirectly and open-endedly through my fiction. I always guard myself against talking about my faith, since talking about it is, however vaguely, a way of proposing it as an outlook, while it is my "in-look." It is something not meant to be discussed; I wake up to my faith in life and my faith in life wakes me up. I would never catalogue it.

I am merely talking philosophically—without being philosophical. And with a clear understanding that these are my speculations about my inner state.

While we all survive on our own, I suspect that a great number of people of my generation share with me—as I do with them—this notion of life as a gift, as the greatest gift there is. *"What is man, that Thou dost make so much of him"* (Job 7:17). Maybe the notion was born during the war so deadly to life . . .

or maybe in the aftermath of war, by living under the soulless Communist system. . . .

1985

JEWS IN THE SOVIET UNION

We must constantly remember that, while Jews in the Soviet Union suffer the deprivation of human rights as much as most of the Soviet Society, they also suffer *additional* deprivation simply because they *are Jews*. They suffer discrimination both collectively—as an ethnic, religious and linguistic minority— and individually—men and women singled out because they are Jewish, and only because they are Jewish.

This denial of basic human rights to Soviet Jews is so flagrant, so brutal, so ingrained in the working of the Soviet totalitarian power structure, that no Jew can escape it. Thus, the tragedy of Soviet Jewry is that it is allowed neither to live in dignity nor allowed to leave to live elsewhere.

In the face of such vast human tragedy, our voice, our pledges and our acts on behalf of Soviet Jewry bring hope of change to the Soviet Jews, to those countless men, women and children who for decades have been trapped in the cage of Soviet hate and oppression, where, for a Jew, even to openly express such hope is already considered an act of treason.

1981

HOSANNA TO WHAT?

To be a Jew in the twentieth century
Is to be offered a gift. If you refuse,
Wishing to be invisible, you choose
Death of the spirit, the stone of insanity.

—MURIEL RUKEYSER

Nearly thirteen years ago, speaking at the opening of the New Haven Holocaust Memorial, built by a city government, and the very first in this country, I said, as one whose own Polish-Jewish family was brutally decimated by the Nazis, that the memorial will serve "as proof of our grief and sorrow and mourning that will never end."

Indeed. In North America, attempts to erect dignified, soul-stirring and unforgettable monuments to the memory of the Holocaust have regrettably evolved into what can only be termed a second Holocaust: a well-meaning, though often inadvertently Jew-demeaning activity, leading to the most aggravated persecution complex in recent Jewish history.

Nowadays, because one third of the world's Jewry perished in the Holocaust, many North American Jews tend to perceive it as Shoah, as an exclusively Jewish disaster. In the words of the President's Commission on the Holocaust (Sept. 27, 1979), "While not all victims were Jews, all Jews were victims solely because they were born Jewish." But at least half of the world's Romanies (unfairly called Gypsies), some 2.5 million Polish Catholics, millions of Soviet citizens and various nationalities were also victims of this genocide, and over 4 million Soviet prisoners of war were gassed in German mobile death units after Stalin refused to exchange them for German POWs.

Almost as if trying to make up for their inaction toward the slaughter of European Jewry during World War II, the Jews of North America turned to the canonization of the Holocaust long after the cannons of that war went silent. Today, this second Holocaust has become our loudest collective cannonade yet. Unfortunately, rather than rejoicing over the sanctity of life and creation as demanded by our Jewish faith, this second Holocaust permeates every aspect of American and Canadian Jewish identity. Its very essence is our inability to find or even to seek spiritual renewal in the life-generating Jewish ethos.

Guided by the second Holocaust, we have begun to perceive ourselves as sainted by our martyrdom in the Nazi ovens—not by our victory over the forces of oppression. We view ourselves not for what we are—as people feted by history—but as ill-fated; not even as chance survivors, but as preordained victims. We insist to ourselves, and to our non-Jewish neighbors, that to be a Jew is synonymous with the Holocaust-bound. We keep on openly shying away from perceiving a Jew as Mark Twain did, as a being whose "contributions to the world's list of great names in literature, science, art, music, finance, medicine, and abstruse learning are also way out of proportion to the weakness of his numbers. He has made a marvelous fight in this world, in all the ages; and has done it with his hands tied behind him."

In our unprecedented self-abnegation, we have reduced, at least in the popular mind, the spiritually opulent history of Jews in dozens of countries to a cultural no-man's-land.

Thus, the second Holocaust dismisses as a mere funeral procession the culturally resplendent thousand-year-old Jewish presence in Poland and Lithuania, the region where, until the Nazi invasion in 1939, the largest Jewish community in the world flourished spiritually for the longest uninterrupted period since biblical times, and from whence originates the majority of the world's Jewry today. And it fails to acknowledge the equally formidable creative panorama of Jewish enlightenment in Russia, the Ukraine, Byelorussia, Armenia and other parts of the Soviet Union where, to this day, lives the world's third-largest Jewish community.

So the Jewish North American obsessive preoccupation with the ashes of the Holocaust continues unchecked, even though the Holocaust could hardly be forgotten by either Jew or Gentile. And rightly so! Today, Holocaust museums can be found in a great many American localities, among them Baltimore, Los Angeles (along with the Beit Hashoa Museum of Tolerance and the Simon Wiesenthal Center), San Francisco, Detroit, and soon in New York City, where the Holocaust Museum of Jewish Heritage is scheduled to open in 1992 to house the archives of the sixteen-year-old Center for Holocaust Studies Documentation and Research.

In addition, a steadily growing number of American communities have Holocaust memorials, Holocaust study centers or research institutes that periodically organize Holocaust observances, conferences, conventions and lectures on all levels.

Furthermore, while many American public schools are required by state laws to teach about the Holocaust, community libraries and study centers provide additional documentation. And the recently published Encyclopedia of the Holocaust (1,905 pages) helps fill any remaining gap in our knowledge.

Last but not least, the United States Holocaust Memorial Museum in Washington, D.C., the biggest and most expensive in the world, is being built on the Mall, next to the Bureau of Printing and Engraving. When it opens in 1993, this museum will display, among other things, the biggest and most expensive collection of Nazi genocidal instruments and remnant possessions of victims and survivors of the Holocaust.

Meanwhile, the International Society for Yad Vashem, a

nondenominational volunteer organization with branches all over the world, seeks funds urgently needed to complete its compelling racism-counteracting projects already commenced at Yad Vashem in Jerusalem.

While Jews of North America remain fixated upon Jewish absence from history—absence, as typified by the Holocaust—this continent lacks, for instance, a single national Jewish Presence Center devoted to Jewish invention and imagination, which have profoundly enriched the human mind.

With North American Jews overly committed to their eulogization of Holocaustica, neo-Nazi-sponsored revisionist historians and the anti-Jewish skinhead morons on some American college campuses and elsewhere, purposefully ignoring facts of history (and not to be impressed by one more impressive Holocaust memorial), effectively poison public opinion with their anti-Jewish vision and their purposely slanted version of the Jewish place in history.

Do we wonder why so many Americans indoctrinated by the second Holocaust (and hence expecting to find disaster at every turn of their own yet-to-be-written history) cannot find Jewish tradition sustaining enough to let them remain—or to become—Jewish?

Is it unusual, then, that last year some half-million American Jews intermarried? That, in steadily growing numbers, the once culturally-minded Jews of North America turn to occultism, possibly as a reaction against the never-ending cult of Holocaustica?

Among the prime victims of this Jewish self-denial count Ladino, the evocative language through which, as much as through Hebrew or Yiddish, millions of Jews around the world for centuries recorded their invigorating thought and literature. Count the Portuguese Synagogue of Amsterdam, which desperately needs restoration. And count the centuries-old Jewish cemetery in Lodz, Poland, where the one-hundred-year-old Jewish funeral home—the largest in the world—keeps vigil over almost two hundred thousand tombstones.

In other parts of Eastern Europe, remains of synagogues, Jewish communal centers, collections of old architectural Jewish blueprints, rare Jewish manuscripts, sculptures, paintings, graphic art and thousands of valuable Jewish books are all pulverized by time simply because most North American Jews no longer seem to care for the preservation of these quintessential treasures of Judaica.

In New England, where once Hebrew was a required course of study at Harvard and Yale as one of the classical languages of both the West and the East, the New England Jewish Music Forum for composers and performers, which for thirty-two years successfully played Jewish music to wide acclaim, is about to be shut down due to the lack of support. This, mind you, in the year when the one-hundredth anniversary of Carnegie Hall is immortalized, as has been music worldwide, by so much Jewish talent!

The second Holocaust also stubbornly continues to suppress the all-embracing, nonsectarian and nonethnocentric roots of Jewish character. This is the very character which, whether giving mankind the Ten Commandments, Irving Berlin's "White Christmas" or George Gershwin's *Porgy and Bess*, always represented a vibrant quest for the celebration of life, Jewish life no less than the life of others. This is the very character which, since our beginning, has always triumphed over death, destruction, ignorance and prejudice.

Remembering the Holocaust and financing Holocaust-related projects that help to make certain that—never again!—such an atrocity could be repeated is clearly one of our most challenging obligations. But that task must not be carried out at the cost of failing to remember—and to make others know—what preceded the Holocaust and what has come after.

1990

RESTORING A POLISH-JEWISH SOUL

Nineteen fifty-seven was a suffocating year for me and my generation. The brief period of cultural freedom of expression ended on a sour note of neo-Stalinist repression. And as if this were not bad enough for Poles already surrounded by the Soviets, Mother Russia had just encircled with her two Sputniks the entire Mother Earth.

Now leap with me over my next thirty years, during which, peacefully writing fiction in America and keeping myself strictly apolitical, for all practical purposes I was effectively excluded from entering Poland: from the day of my departure, since I failed to return in the prescribed time, then as *persona non grata*, as a result of what Polish propaganda said about me and my first novel, *The Painted Bird*. With the passing years, my father died, then my mother—my last blood relative—survived by my adopted brother, without me at their side. Enough said?

Knowing I was away from Poland for over thirty *non-grata* years, imagine how grateful I felt when I heard the following request from the American Foundation for Polish-Jewish Studies, of which I am the board chairman:

Will I deliver a Judaica Award to the most Polish Judaica-preserving Polish-Gentile and deliver it personally to him in Warsaw? To this request my Self says yes.

Next, I pay a semi-formal call on the Polish Consul in New York. Feigning nonchalance, though my native heart is racing, I talk in Polish, which I have kept alive even though since 1957 I have expressed my inner syntax in English. Point-blank I ask him: Would the Polish Government mind if I were to visit Poland?

The Polish Government would not mind, answers the Polish Consul. In fact, he goes on, since Mr. Kosinski had once before visited Poland, from 1933 when he was born there until 1957, when he chose America for his creative exile, the current Polish Government would treat his trip as a re-visitation, not a visit, he says with a straight face.

Packing in my knapsack a pack of memory chips loaded with memories unchipped by time, I take off for Poland accompanied by Kiki, my American-born, British-educated wife, who does not speak one word of Polish.

We touch down in Warsaw after a brief flight from Vienna— and "by speaking Polish to anyone I choose, my touchdown in Poland touches the deepest me," I promptly cable my American Self already from the Warsaw airport, swallowing a capsule of tears.

On the day of our arrival, what was initially planned in Warsaw as a small Judaica Award reception becomes, by chance, a loud public event. Anywhere I turn, I am interviewed, be it by the playful Solidarity organists, or by the ever-so-serious Party organs.

Following the dictates of heart and memory, I travel with my wife from place to place, mixing moments of surprise with doses of time-altered recognition. And then we travel to Lodz, my hometown.

Until World War II, Lodz, a textile center, was called "the

Manchester of Eastern Europe," where some 250,000 spiritually inspired, mostly Yiddish-speaking Jews constituted one third of the city's entire population, and where I was born. I lived here before the war and studied here after.

As I walk through the city's streets my reconnaissance of Lodz turns into a reconnaissance of my Self.

What impresses me most is the Jewish cemetery—the largest in the world. Over 180,000 family graves and mausolea proudly keep vigil here—many of them among the largest and most elaborate I have ever seen. It was in the Lodz ghetto where many of my relatives perished, either here or on the way to the gas chambers.

Back to the present. All tense, I meet Henryk, my adopted brother. Remember that, when I saw him last, back in 1957, he was seventeen years old. He is now some forty-seven. With thirty years in between, he still looks the same to me.

While in the intervening years, with the Iron Curtain intervening, Henryk and I seldom talked on the phone or wrote to one another, now—arm in arm, tear in tear—we bend in double sorrow over the double grave of our parents.

After meeting Henryk, my restless Self selflessly takes me and Kiki from Lodz to Kazimierz.

Once a separate entity inhabited for many centuries mostly by Polish Jews, today Kazimierz forms an inseparable part of Krakow, from where Polish kings ruled the Polish commonwealth, mighty enough to grant millions of Jews from elsewhere their *polin*—from the Hebrew word *pohlin* ("here shalt thou lodge in exile")—as Jews kept on calling Poland while first calling upon it.

In Kazimierz, in the old Jewish quarter where so many houses and synagogues stand in need of repair, as I take photographs of the sixteenth-century Jewish Remo cemetery, I hear every stone screaming at me: "Restore Jewish Kazimierz, and do it quick; am I not part of your very soul?"

Soulfully leaving behind the spiritually luminous soil of Krakow, in less than an hour Kiki and I pause at Auschwitz, the man-made hell, where the Nazis tried to turn the all-fertile Jewish soul into a fertilizer—and failed miserably. Enough said.

With short fragments of my novels already appearing in the Polish press, I accept ad hoc invitations to address mostly student audiences. I talk to them spontaneously; spontaneously, they talk back to me. Selfishly, I boast to them about how it feels to have my Self engaged again by Polish language after thirty years of thinking in English.

Selflessly, they tell me what it feels like for them—young and well-educated—to be forced to wait from twenty to fifty years for an apartment, some fifteen million of which are desperately needed in Poland now.

Hearing this, I promptly cable my American Self: "Start in Poland a profitable Pax Americana."

When I am about to leave Poland, my Polish-Jewish Self cables me another self-addressed question: "What kind of Poles did you meet in Poland?"

As one who collects impressions as others collect Impressionists, I answer: "Most of the Poles I encountered were born after World War II and after 1968, the year a few infamous Party thugs forced the remaining Jews out of Poland."

And then I add a one-thousand-year-old afterthought: "With so much Jewish cultural legacy steaming from the spiritually fertile Polish soil, to these young men and women the Polish-Jewish relations are a mystery—mystery, not stigmata. They are as prompted to know me better as I am eager to know them."

Now you know why, rejuvenated by what I found within myself during my twelve days in Poland, I started a new romance with my one-thousand-year-old Polish-Jewish soul. Enough said?

1988

SPEAKING
FOR MY SELF

There, *in Eastern Europe, the Jewish people came into its own. It did not live like a guest in somebody else's house, who must constantly keep in mind the ways and customs of the host. There Jews lived without reservation and without disguise, outside their homes no less than within them.* I read with my inner eye what Abraham Joshua Heschel, my Jewish spiritual teacher, says in *The Earth Is the Lord's: The Inner World of the Jew in Eastern Europe,* when my outer eye catches a phrase "Polish anti-Semitism" on a page of a local American newspaper.

Instantly, my Jewish Soul steps out from its niche and summons the plenary session of my inner kahal, a committee of scholars and spiritual oligarchs, gathering the minute I sit down at my typewriter. Speaking in the voice of my Polish-Jewish mother, my Soul opens the session by literally opening herself up.

"As long as anti-Semitism signifies a racist hatred of Judaism, of everything and everyone Jewish—hatred, that illness of the spirit, not a momentary antagonism, opposition or spiritual ill-feeling—the phrase 'Polish anti-Semitism' strikes me as a spiritual contradiction.

"To start with, until World War II, until the Holocaust,

both of which claimed the lives of so many Jews who were Polish nationals, as well as Poles, the Jews had lived in Poland for a longer time than in any other country with the exception of ancient Israel," says my Soul, who now says it in the voice of my Polish-Jewish father.

"Only in Poland, with the exception of ancient Israel, of course, were Jews free to develop, nourish and cultivate their Jewish religion. And, may I ask you," addressing every member of my kahal, my Soul now speaks up with a voice of my own, "doesn't our Jewish religion matter to us most?"

"Hear! Hear! Hear O'Israel!" shout one after another the members of my kahal.

"Don't just hear me out. Hear Simon Dubnow, the Jewish historian. He says, and I quote, '*Hassidism represents one of the most significant and most original phenomena not only in the history of Judaism, but also in the history of the development of religions in general* . . .' and he says this about the Hassidic movement which, ever since it was born in Poland, has been the greatest spiritual revival in our four-thousand-year-old Jewish history!"

"Now," my Soul goes on, "had Poles harbored hate for the Jews, had they been racists, that is, anti-Semites, would they let the Polish Jews cultivate for centuries right in their very midst, such a most significant Jewish spiritual phenomenon? They would not! Enough said." Ending her soulful remarks, my Soul withdraws into her most private recess. Time for others to take to the floor.

"I could not agree with you more, my dear Soul," says the next speaker, the learned Rabbi of Apt, so named after Apt, a town in Poland where, like most Polish Jews in Poland, he once lived in a small, crowded apartment. Just as well, since, in English, the word apt stands for quick to learn, and is also an abbreviation for the word apartment.

"Let me remind you of what I believe," says the learned rabbi. "I believe in the transmigration of souls. Transmigration, not emigration. I was the one who first proposed that, far from being the product of *creatio ex nihilo*, one's soul is the creation of one's past. Hence, to know what kind of Jew are you today, you must first find out where your Jewish soul was yesterday. By yesterday I mean centuries. Who knows such things better than we, the migrating Polish-Jewish souls?"

"Hear! Hear! Hear O'Israel," others unanimously agree.

"For hundreds of years, our Jewish soul lived right next door to, and I might add, often with, the Polish soul. The troubles they had with one another—and troubles they were!—stemmed from spiritual proximity, from closeness, not from distance. From spiritual fusion as much as from historical and economic confusion. In brief, they stemmed from Polish-Jewish relations—with the word relation signifying here kinship, i.e., one's closest relations, not only a narration. How could the Poles, who for centuries remained the closest relatives of the Jews, be anti-Semitic? Speak then, if you must, of certain wrongs committed against the Jews by the Poles, but when you do, remember that during the long period of some thousand years, Poles were most generous hosts to their Jewish neighbors, in spite of being themselves troubled by their troublesome Russian, Prussian and Austro-Hungarian neighbors who suddenly turned into their hosts. Speak then, if you so choose of the anti-Jewish outbursts, of violent, often brutal flare-ups. Mention, if you have to, political, ethnic, or religious paroxysms and seizures, but whenever you speak about these spiritually charged Polish-Jewish relations please mention the existence of the most generous and agreeable Polish national soul." The Rabbi of Apt sits down all flushed.

The next speaker is Father Augustine, an American-Polish priest whose name in the Old Country was Augustynski. He is the distinguished literary critic who rightly declared most of my novels to be confessional in nature, stemming, no doubt, from

my surviving the war among Polish Catholics who first introduced me to the confessional and to confession. At my inner
university Father Augustynski chairs—you guessed it!—the
chair of confessional literature.

"I confess that I wholeheartedly concur with Rabbi Apt, my
learned predecessor," says Father Augustynski and he says it *ex
cathedra*.

"Some of the greatest Polish spiritual works, literary as well
as scholarly, were written by the Jews in Poland who, having
passed the Polish Aptitude Test with highest honors, often
wrote them in exquisite Polish, a language they knew and wor-
shipped more than anyone else," says Father Augustine. "I know
it for a fact since, figuratively speaking, I was often their father
confessor." Having said this, Father Augustine gives the next
speaker enough space to confess to what he terms "the always
most widely open Polish-Jewish confessional."

"I bet on this confessional my entire oral Jewish narrative
tradition, and my Polish-American novelistic calling," says Mr.
Scribe. "Knowing what I know about these Polish folks," Mr.
Scribe goes on, "I top this bet with my undeniable knowledge
of Polish literary folklore."

Now, in case you don't know his name, Mr. Scribe is the
fifty-four-year-old Polish-born American writer who, having
once written in Poland some scholarly works in Polish, his
mother tongue, since the age of twenty-four has written only
in the English language—a writing instrument he calls his
stepmother's tongue. Parenthetically, I add that Mr. Scribe's
original Jewish name was Sopher, a name his parents first
changed to Skryba.

"Had Poles been anti-Semitic, would they let the Jews create
Yiddish, their own separate language? I mean separate from
Polish. Would they let the Jews speak Yiddish and not just to
speak but talk in it often nonstop, as if, pardon this anti-Jewish

expression, the Polish language wasn't by itself good enough for them? That very rich Polish language which I still know and love?" asks Mr. Scribe passionately. "Keep in mind that, for centuries, Yiddish has been a language of the Jewish soul, a veritable Jewish mother tongue. Now what can be more important to a Jew than his Jewish mother—or his mother's tongue?" Here, my Soul speaks in unison with the double-jointed soul of my Sephardic father and my Ashkenazim mother, and both souls speak to me from my most innermost transmigrational well.

"Isn't Hebrew a Jewish mother tongue?" mechanically asks my inner non-Jewish Word Processor.

"It certainly is. But so is Yiddish. Clearly, the Jewish mother speaks to her Soul—and hears from her—in two languages," says my Soul, who is herself bilingual. "Don't just listen to me. Listen to what Abraham Joshua Heschel had to say. Heschel, that most famous Jewish-American theologian who, himself born in Warsaw, took his entire name from the Rabbi of Apt, and with it inherited some of his soul. Says Heschel, and he says it for everyone to hear. "Further, the East European Jews created their own language, Yiddish, which was born out of a will to make intelligible, to explain and simplify the tremendous complexities of the sacred literature. Thus there arose, as though spontaneously, *a mother tongue* . . . The Jews have spoken many languages since they went into exile; this was the only one they called 'Jewish.' "

The Soul ends her pointed remarks and returns to her seat in the row of reunited souls. The next speaker is my Memory, who rushes to the podium with the textbook *History of World War II* and my family album in hand.

"Throughout the Nazi occupation, throughout the horror of the Holocaust, Poles faced biological extermination, not so much less than the Jews," says my Memory, raising the textbook and the album with her hand high above the podium for everyone to see. "Could a Jew, one who owes his very life, his very being, to his Polish Catholic saviors, ever think about them as being anti-Semitic?" She raises her voice for everyone to hear.

Now my inner Actor takes to the floor. Even though he is a Russian, he was born in Poland with an old Jewish-Polish soul. He starts his speech by reminding everyone that they might have caught sight of him when he portrayed the shaken and shaken-up Comrade Grigori Zinoviev, Lenin's emissary, vis-à-vis John Reed, the American writer who in 1919 wrote *Ten Days That Shook the World,* and portrayed him true to life in *Red,* Warren Beatty's Hollywood-made world-shaking American revolutionary movie.

"Your very looks speak for the Polish bravery. The bravery of the Poles who, in spite of your looks, sheltered you during the Holocaust! The bravery of the Poles who risked for you their very lives—in spite of your looks!" He sounds like a Soviet World War II commissar who in 1945 had liberated me, as well as my country, and in such a way was instrumental in the creation of my inner kahal.

"Would you please be more specific?" my Vanity asks.

"Don't ask, look!" Curling his lips with well-acted distaste, Zinoviev looks at my curly hair as if I were a black sheep. "Look at his nose! In case you can't see it, his nose comes straight from a camel and by this I don't mean a straight American Camel cigarette. Hear O'Israel!" Zinoviev tactlessly sticks his finger in my already twisted inner ear. "Now that you have given him a good look, tell me," he goes on. "Could a Jewish kid looking like that ever pass for a Polish goy? He could not. Not in a thousand years!" he says, staring me in the face as if indeed I were a six-year-old.

The discussion is over. One after another the assorted oligarchs cast their view—views, rather than votes. Finally, taking their views into full account, my Self takes the stand. Now everyone quiets down, and for a good reason. My Self governs—governs, as well as runs—my entire inner state and estate.

"The evidence of Jewish stay in Poland *led to the conclusion that in this period our people attained the highest degree of inwardness. I feel justified in saying that it was the golden period in Jewish history, in the history of the Jewish soul."* Unabashedly my Self quotes Abraham Joshua Heschel, his spiritual *guru.*

Then standing up in full view of the entire kahal, he ends the plenum by saying, "And I hereby declare the phrase 'Polish anti-Semitism' as a non-spiritual *persona non grata.*"

1987

TIME OF LIFE, TIME OF ART

AFTERWARD:
THE PAINTED BIRD
TENTH ANNIVERSARY
EDITION (1976)

In the spring of 1963, I visited Switzerland with my American-born wife, Mary. We had vacationed there before, but were now in the country for a different purpose: my wife had been battling a supposedly incurable illness for months and had come to Switzerland to consult yet another group of specialists. Since we expected to remain for some time, we had taken a suite in a palatial hotel that dominated the lakefront of a fashionable old resort.

Among the permanent residents at the hotel was a clique of wealthy Western Europeans who had come to the town just before the outbreak of World War II. They had all abandoned their homelands before the slaughter actually began and they never had to fight for their lives. Once ensconced in their Swiss haven, self-preservation for them meant no more than living from day to day. Most of them were in their seventies and eighties, aimless pensioners obsessively talking about getting old, growing steadily less able or willing to leave the hotel grounds. They spent their time in the lounges and restaurants or strolling through the private park. I often followed them, pausing when they did before portraits of statesmen who had visited the hotel between the wars; I read with them the somber plaques commemorating various international peace conferences that had been held in the hotel's convention halls after World War I.

Occasionally I would chat with a few of these voluntary exiles, but whenever I alluded to the war years in Central or Eastern Europe, they never failed to remind me that, because they had come to Switzerland before the violence began, they knew the war only vaguely, through radio and newspaper reports. Referring to one country in which most of the extermination camps had been located, I pointed out that between 1939 and 1945 only a million people had died as the result of direct military action, but five and a half million had been exterminated by the invaders. Over three million victims were Jews, and one third of them were under sixteen. These losses worked out to two hundred and twenty deaths per thousand people, and no one would ever be able to compute how many others were mutilated, traumatized, broken in health or spirit. My listeners nodded politely, admitting that they had always believed that reports about the camps and gas chambers had been much embellished by overwrought reporters. I assured them that, having spent my childhood and adolescence during the war and postwar years in Eastern Europe, I knew that real events had been more brutal than the most bizarre fantasies.

On days when my wife was confined to the clinic for treatment, I would hire a car and drive, with no destination in mind. I cruised along smartly manicured Swiss roads winding through fields which bristled with squat steel and concrete tank traps planted during the war to impede advancing tanks. They still stood, a crumbling defense against an invasion that was never launched, as out of place and purposeless as the antiquated exiles at the hotel.

Many afternoons I rented a boat and rowed aimlessly on the lake. During those moments I experienced my isolation intensely: my wife, the emotional link to my existence in the

United States, was dying. I could contact what remained of my family in Eastern Europe only through infrequent, cryptic letters, always at the mercy of the censor.

As I drifted across the lake, I felt haunted by a sense of hopelessness—not merely loneliness, or the fear of my wife's death, but a sense of anguish directly connected to the emptiness of the exiles' lives and the ineffectiveness of the postwar peace conferences. As I thought of the plaques that adorned the hotel walls, I questioned whether the authors of peace treaties had signed them in good faith. The events that followed the conferences did not support such a conjecture. Yet the aging exiles in the hotel continued to believe that the war had been some inexplicable aberration in a world of well-intentioned politicians whose humanitarianism could not be challenged. They could not accept that certain guarantors of peace had later become the initiators of war. Because of this disbelief, millions like my parents and myself, lacking any chance to escape, had been forced to experience events far worse than those that the treaties so grandiloquently prohibited.

The extreme discrepancy between the facts as I knew them and the exiles' and diplomats' hazy, unrealistic view of the world bothered me intensely. I began to reexamine my past and decided to turn from my studies of social science to fiction. Unlike politics, which offered only extravagant promises of a utopian future, I knew fiction could present lives as they are truly lived.

When I had come to America six years before this European visit, I was determined never again to set foot in the country where I had spent the war years. That I had survived was due solely to chance, and I had always been acutely aware that hundreds of thousands of other children had been condemned. But although I felt strongly about that injustice, I did not perceive myself as a vendor of personal guilt and private reminiscences, nor as a chronicler of the disaster that befell my people and my generation, but purely as a storyteller.

TIME OF LIFE, TIME OF ART

". . . the truth is the only thing in which people do not differ. Everyone is subconsciously mastered by the spiritual will to live, by the aspiration to live at any cost; one wants to live because one lives, because the whole world lives . . ." wrote a Jewish concentration camp inmate shortly before his death in the gas chamber. "We are here in the company of death," wrote another inmate. "They tattoo the newcomers. Everyone gets his number. From that moment on you have lost your 'self' and have become transformed into a number. You no longer are what you were before, but a worthless moving number . . . We are approaching our new graves . . . iron discipline reigns here in the camp of death. Our brain has grown dull, the thoughts are numbered: it is not possible to grasp this new language . . ."

My purpose in writing a novel was to examine "this new language" of brutality and its consequent new counter-language of anguish and despair. The book would be written in English, in which I had already written two works of social psychology, having relinquished my mother tongue when I abandoned my homeland. Moreover, as English was still new to me, I could write dispassionately, free from the emotional connotation one's native language always contains.

As the story began to evolve, I realized that I wanted to extend certain themes, modulating them through a series of five novels. This five-book cycle would present archetypal aspects of the individual's relationship to society. The first book of the cycle was to deal with the most universally accessible of these societal metaphors: man would be portrayed in his most vulnerable state, as a child, and society in its most deadly form, in a state of war. I hoped the confrontation between the defenseless individual and overpowering society, between the child and war, would represent the essential anti-human condition.

Furthermore, it seemed to me, novels about childhood demand the ultimate act of imaginative involvement. Since we have no direct access to that most sensitive, earliest period of our lives, we must re-create it before we can begin to assess our present selves. Although all novels force us into such an act of transference, making us experience ourselves as different beings, it is generally more difficult to imagine ourselves as children than as adults.

As I began to write, I recalled *The Birds*, the satirical play by Aristophanes. His protagonists, based on important citizens of ancient Athens, were made anonymous in an idyllic natural realm, "a land of easy and fair rest, where man can sleep safely and grow feathers." I was struck by the pertinence and universality of the setting Aristophanes had provided more than two millennia ago.

Aristophanes' symbolic use of birds, which allowed him to deal with actual events and characters without the restrictions which the writing of history imposes, seemed particularly appropriate, as I associated it with a peasant custom I had witnessed during my childhood. One of the villagers' favorite entertainments was trapping birds, painting their feathers, then releasing them to rejoin their flock. As these brightly colored creatures sought the safety of their fellows, the other birds, seeing them as threatening aliens, attacked and tore at the outcasts until they killed them. I decided I too would set my work in a mythic domain, in the timeless fictive present, unrestrained by geography or history. My novel would be called *The Painted Bird*

Because I saw myself solely as a storyteller, the first edition of *The Painted Bird* carried only minimal information about me and I refused to give any interviews. Yet this very stand placed me in a position of conflict. Well-intentioned writers, critics and readers sought facts to back up their claims that the novel was autobiographical. They wanted to cast me in the role of spokesman for my generation, especially for those who had survived the war; but for me survival was an individual action that earned the survivor the right to speak only for himself. Facts about my life and my origins, I felt, should not be used to test the book's authenticity, any more than they should be used to encourage readers to read *The Painted Bird*.

Furthermore, I felt then, as I do now, that fiction and autobiography are very different modes. Autobiography emphasizes a single life: the reader is invited to become the observer of another man's existence and encouraged to compare his own life to the subject's. A fictional life, on the other hand, forces the reader to contribute: he does not simply compare; he actually enters a fictional role, expanding it in terms of his own experience, his own creative and imaginative powers.

I remained determined that the novel's life be independent of mine. I objected when many foreign publishers refused to issue *The Painted Bird* without including, as a preface or as an epilogue, excerpts from my personal correspondence with one of my first foreign-language publishers. They hoped that these excerpts would soften the book's impact. I had written these letters in order to explain, rather than mitigate, the novel's vision; thrust between the book and its readers, they violated the novel's integrity, interjecting my immediate presence into a work intended to stand by itself. The paperback version of *The Painted Bird*, which followed a year after the original, contained no biographical information at all. Perhaps it was because of this that many school reading lists placed Kosinski not among contemporary writers, but among the deceased.

After *The Painted Bird's* publication in the United States and in Western Europe (it was not published in my homeland until 1989, nor allowed across its borders), certain Eastern European newspapers and magazines launched a campaign against it. Despite their ideological differences, many journals attacked the same passages from the novel (usually quoted out of context) and altered sequences to support their accusations. Outraged editorials in state-controlled publications charged that American authorities had assigned me to write *The Painted Bird* for covert political purposes. These publications, ostensibly unaware that every book published in the United States must be registered by the Library of Congress, even cited the Library catalogue number as conclusive evidence that the United States Government had subsidized the book. Conversely, the anti-Soviet periodicals singled out the positive light in which, they claimed, I had portrayed the Russian soldiers, as proof that the book attempted to justify the Soviet presence in Eastern Europe.

Most Eastern European condemnation focused on the novel's alleged specificity. Although I had made sure that the names of people and places I used could not be associated exclusively with any national group, my critics accused *The Painted Bird* of being a libelous documentary of life in identifiable communities during the Second World War. Some detractors even insisted that my references to folklore and native customs, so brazenly detailed, were caricatures of their particular home provinces. Still others attacked the novel for distorting native lore, for defaming the peasant character, and for reinforcing the propaganda weapons of the region's enemies.

As I later learned, these diverse criticisms were part of a large-scale attempt by an extreme nationalist group to create a feeling of danger and disruption within my homeland, a plot intended to force the remaining Jewish population to leave the state. The *New York Times* reported that *The Painted Bird* was being denounced as propaganda by reactionary forces "seeking an armed showdown with Eastern Europe." Ironically, the novel began to assume a role not unlike that of its protagonist, the boy, a native who has become an alien, a Gypsy who is believed to command destructive forces and to be able to cast spells over all who cross his path.

The campaign against the book, which had been generated in the capital of the country, soon spread throughout the nation. Within a few weeks, several hundred articles and an avalanche of gossip items appeared. The state-controlled television network commenced a series, "In the Footsteps of *The Painted Bird*," presenting interviews with persons who had supposedly came in contact with me or my family during the war years. The interviewer would read a passage from *The Painted Bird*, then produce a person he claimed was the individual on whom the fictional character was based. As these disoriented, often uneducated witnesses were brought forward, horrified at what they were supposed to have done, they angrily denounced the book and its author.

One of Eastern Europe's most accomplished and revered authors read *The Painted Bird* in its French translation and praised the novel in his review. Government pressure soon forced him to recant. He published his revised opinion, then followed it with an "Open Letter to Jerzy Kosinski," which appeared in the literary magazine he himself edited. In it, he warned me that I, like another prizewinning novelist who had betrayed his native language for an alien tongue and the praise of the decadent West, would end my days by cutting my throat in some seedy hotel on the Riviera.

At the time of the publication of *The Painted Bird*, my mother, my only surviving blood relative, was in her sixties and had undergone two operations for cancer. When the leading local newspaper discovered she was still living in the city where I had been born, it printed scurrilous articles referring to her as the mother of a renegade, inciting local zealots and crowds of enraged townspeople to descend upon her house. Summoned by my mother's nurse, the police arrived but stood idly by, only pretending to control the vigilantes.

When an old school friend telephoned me in New York to tell me, guardedly, what was happening, I mobilized whatever support I could from international organizations, but for months it seemed to do little good, for the angry townspeople, none of whom had actually seen my book, continued their attacks. Finally government officials, embarrassed by pressures brought by concerned organizations outside the country, ordered the municipal authorities to move my mother to another town. She remained there for a few weeks until the assaults died down, then moved to the capital, leaving everything behind her. With the help of certain friends, I was able to keep informed about her whereabouts and to get money to her regularly.

Although most of her family had been exterminated in the country which now persecuted her, my mother refused to emigrate, insisting that she wanted to die and be buried next to my father, in the land where she had been born and where all her people had perished. When she did die, her death was made an occasion of shame and a warning to her friends. No public announcement of the funeral was permitted by the authorities, and the simple death notice was not published until several days after her burial.

In the United States, press reports of these foreign attacks provoked a flood of anonymous threatening letters from naturalized Eastern Europeans, who felt I had slandered their countrymen and maligned their ethnic heritage. Almost none of the nameless letter writers seemed to have actually read *The Painted Bird*; most of them merely parroted the Eastern European attacks carried secondhand in émigré publications.

One day when I was alone in my Manhattan apartment, the bell rang. Assuming it was a delivery I expected, I immediately opened the door. Two burly men in heavy raincoats pushed me into the room, slamming the door shut behind them. They pinned me against the wall and examined me closely. Apparently confused, one of them pulled a newspaper clipping from his pocket. It was the *New York Times* article about the Eastern European attacks against *The Painted Bird*, and it contained a blurred reproduction of an old photograph of me. My attackers, shouting something about *The Painted Bird*, began threatening to beat me with lengths of steel pipe wrapped in newspaper, which they produced from inside their coat sleeves. I protested that I was not the author; the man in the photograph, I said, was my cousin for whom I was often mistaken. I added that he had just stepped out but would be returning any minute. As they sat down on the couch to wait, still holding their weapons, I asked the men what they wanted. One of them replied that they had come to punish Kosinski for *The Painted Bird*, a book that vilified their country and ridiculed their people. Though they lived in the United States, he assured me, they were patriots. Soon the other man joined in, railing against Kosinski, lapsing into the rural dialect I recalled so well. I kept silent, studying their broad peasant faces, their stocky bodies, the poorly fitting raincoats. A generation removed from thatched huts, rank marsh grasses, and ox-drawn plows, they were still the peasants I had known. They seemed to have stepped out of the pages of *The Painted Bird*, and for a moment I felt very possessive about the pair. If indeed they were my characters, it was only natural that they should come to visit me, so I amicably offered them vodka which, after an initial reluctance, they eagerly accepted. As they drank, I began to tidy up the loose items on my bookshelves, then quite casually drew a small revolver from behind the two-volume *Dictionary of Americanisms* that stood at the end of a shelf. I told the men to drop their weapons and raise their hands; as soon as they obeyed, I picked up my camera. Revolver in one hand, camera in the other, I quickly took half a dozen photos. These snapshots, I announced, would prove the men's identity, if ever I decided to press charges for forced entry and attempted assault. They begged me to spare them; after all, they pleaded, they had not harmed me or Kosinski. I pretended to reflect on that, and finally responded that, since their images had been preserved, I had no more reason to detain them in the flesh.

That was not the only incident in which I felt the repercussions of the Eastern European smear campaign. On several occasions I was accosted outside my apartment house or in my garage. Three or four times strangers recognized me on the street and offered hostile or insulting remarks. At a concert honoring a pianist born in my homeland, a covey of patriotic old ladies attacked me with their umbrellas, while screeching absurdly dated invectives. Even now, ten years after *The Painted Bird*'s publication, citizens of my former country, where the novel remains banned, still accuse me of treachery, tragically unaware that by consciously deceiving them, the government continues to feed their prejudices, rendering them victims of the same forces from which my protagonist, the boy, so narrowly escaped.

About a year after the publication of *The Painted Bird*, P.E.N., an international literary association, contacted me regarding a young poet from my homeland. She had come to America for complicated heart surgery, which, unfortunately, had not accomplished all the doctors had hoped it would. She did not speak English and P.E.N. told me she needed assistance in the first months after the operation. She was still in her early twenties, but had already published several volumes of poetry and was regarded as one of her country's most promising young writers. I had known and admired her work for some years, and was pleased at the prospect of meeting her.

During the weeks while she recuperated in New York we wandered through the city. I often photographed her, using Manhattan's park and skyscrapers as a backdrop. We became close friends and she applied for an extension to her visa, but the consulate refused to renew it. Unwilling to abandon her language and her family permanently, she had no choice but to return home. Later, I received a letter from her, through a third person, in which she warned me that the national writers' union had learned of our intimacy and was now demanding that she write a short story based on her New York encounter with the author of *The Painted Bird*. The story would portray me as a man devoid of morals, a pervert who had sworn to denigrate all that her motherland stood for. At first she had refused to write it; she told them that, because she knew no English, she had never read *The Painted Bird*, nor had she ever discussed politics with me. But her colleagues continued to remind her that the writers' union had made possible her surgery and was paying for all her post-operative medical attention. They insisted that, as she was a prominent poet, and as she had considerable influence among the young, she was duty-bound to fulfill her patriotic obligation and attack, in print, the man who had betrayed her country.

Friends sent me the weekly literary magazine which published the required defamatory story she had written. I tried to reach her through our mutual friends to tell her that I understood she had been maneuvered into a position from which there was no escape, but she never responded. Some months later I heard that she had had a fatal heart attack.

Whether the reviews praised or damned the novel, Western criticism of *The Painted Bird* always contained an undertone of uneasiness. Most American and British critics objected to my descriptions of the boy's experiences on the grounds that they dwelt too deeply on cruelty. Many tended to dismiss the author as well as the novel, claiming that I had exploited the horrors of war to satisfy my own peculiar imagination. On the occasion of the twenty-fifth anniversary observances of the National Book Awards, a respected contemporary American novelist wrote that books like *The Painted Bird*, with their unrelieved brutality, did not bode well for the future of the English-language novel. Other critics argued that the book was merely a work of personal reminiscence; they insisted that, given the raw materials of war-torn Eastern Europe, anyone could concoct a plot overflowing with brutal drama.

In point of fact, almost none of those who chose to view the book as a historical novel bothered to refer to actual source materials. Personal accounts of survivors and official war documents were either unknown by or irrelevant to my critics. None seemed to have taken the time to read the easily available testimony, such as that of a nineteen-year-old survivor describing the punishment meted out to an Eastern European village that had sheltered an enemy of the Reich: "I witnessed how the Germans arrived together with the Kalmuks to pacify the village," she wrote. "It was a terrible scene, one that will live in my memory until I die. After the village was surrounded, they began raping the women, then a command was given to burn it together with all the inhabitants. The excited barbarians took firebrands to the houses and those who ran away were shot at or forced back to the flames. They grabbed small children from their mothers and threw them into the fire. And when the grief-stricken women ran to save their children, they would shoot them first in one leg and then in the other. Only after they had suffered would they kill them. That orgy lasted all day. In the evening, after the Germans left, the villagers slowly crawled back to the village to save its remnants. What we saw was awful: the smoldering timbers, and in the approaches to the cottages the remains of the burned. The fields behind the village were covered with the dead; here, a mother with a child in her arms, its brains splashed across her face; there, a ten-year-old with his schoolbook in his hand. All the dead were buried in five mass graves." Every village of Eastern Europe knew of such events, and hundreds of settlements had suffered similar fates.

In other documents, a concentration camp commander unhesitatingly admitted that "the rule was to kill children right away as they were too young to work." Another commandant stated that within forty-seven days he had ready for shipment to Germany almost one hundred thousand pieces of clothing belonging to Jewish children who had been gassed. A diary left by a Jewish gas chamber attendant recorded that "of the hundred Gypsies to die in the camp every day, more than half were children." And another Jewish attendant described the SS guards nonchalantly feeling the sexual parts of every adolescent girl who passed on her way to the gas chambers.

Perhaps the best proof that I was not overstating the brutality and cruelty that characterized the war years in Eastern Europe is the fact that some of my old school friends, who had succeeded in obtaining contraband copies of *The Painted Bird*, wrote that the novel was a pastoral tale compared with the experiences so many of them and their relatives had endured during the war. They blamed me for watering down historical truth and accused me of pandering to an Anglo-Saxon sensibility whose only confrontation with national cataclysm had been the Civil War a century earlier, when bands of abandoned children roamed through the devastated South.

It was difficult for me to object to this kind of criticism. In 1938, some sixty members of my family attended the last of our annual reunions. Among them were distinguished scholars, philanthropists, physicians, lawyers and financiers. Of this number, only three persons survived the war. Furthermore my mother and father had lived through the First World War, the Russian Revolution, and the repression of minorities during the twenties and thirties. Almost every year in which they had lived was marked by suffering, divided families, the mutilation and death of loved ones, but even they, who had witnessed so much, were unprepared for the savagery unleashed in 1939.

Throughout World War II, they were in constant danger. Forced almost daily to seek new hiding places, their existence became one of fear, flight, and hunger; dwelling always among strangers, submerging themselves into others' lives in order to disguise their own, gave rise to an unending sense of uprootedness. My mother later told me that, even when they were physically safe, they were constantly tortured by the possibility that their decision to send me away had been wrong, that I would have been safer with them. There were no words, she said, to describe their anguish as they saw young children being herded into the trains bound for the ovens or the horrendous special camps scattered throughout the country.

It was therefore very much for their sakes and for people like them that I wanted to write fiction which would reflect, and perhaps exorcise, the horrors that they had found so inexpressible.

After my father's death, my mother gave me the hundreds of small notebooks he had kept during the war. Even in flight, she said, never really believing that he would survive, my father somehow managed to make extensive notes on his studies of higher mathematics in a delicate, miniature script. He was primarily a philologist and classicist, but during the war only mathematics offered him relief from quotidian reality. Only by enveloping himself in the realm of pure logic, abstracting himself from the world of letters with its implicit commentary on human affairs, could my father transcend the hideous events that surrounded him daily.

Once my father was dead, my mother sought in me some reflection of his characteristics and temperament. She was primarily concerned over the fact that, unlike my father, I had chosen to express myself publicly through writing. Throughout his life my father had consistently refused to speak in public, to lecture, to write books or articles, because he believed in the sanctity of privacy. To him the most rewarding life was one passed unnoticed by the world. He was convinced that the creative individual, whose art draws the world to him, pays for the success of his work with his own happiness and that of his loved ones.

My father's desire for anonymity was part of a lifelong attempt to construct his own philosophical system to which no one else would have access. I, for whom exclusion and anonymity had been a fact of daily life as a boy, conversely felt compelled to create a world of fiction to which all had access.

Despite his mistrust of the written word, it was my father who had first unwittingly steered me toward writing in English. After my arrival in the United States, displaying the same patience and precision with which he had kept his notebooks, he began a series of daily letters to me that contained intensively detailed explanations of the finer points of English grammar and idiom. These lessons, typed on airmail paper with a philologist's concern for accuracy, contained no personal or local news. There was probably little that life had not already taught me, my father claimed, and he had no fresh insights to pass on to his son.

By that time my father had sustained several serious heart attacks, and his failing sight had reduced his field of vision to an image area about the size of a quarto page. He knew his life was coming to an end, and he must have felt that the only gift he could give me was his own knowledge of the English language, refined and enriched by a lifetime of study.

Only when I knew I would never see him again did I realize how well he had known me and how much he loved me. He took great pains to formulate every lesson according to my particular cast of mind. The examples of English usage that he selected were always from poets and writers I admired, and consistently dealt with topics and ideas of special interest to me.

My father died before *The Painted Bird* was published, never seeing the book to which he had contributed so much. Now, as I reread his letters, I realize the extent of my father's wisdom: he wanted to bequeath to me a voice that could guide me through a new country. This legacy, he must have hoped, would free me to participate fully in the land where I had chosen to make my future.

The late sixties saw a loosening of social and artistic constraints in the United States, and colleges and schools began to adopt *The Painted Bird* as supplementary reading in modern literature courses. Students and teachers frequently wrote to me, and I was sent copies of term papers and essays dealing with the book. To many of my young readers, its characters and events paralleled people and situations in their own lives; it offered a topography for those who perceived the world as a battle between the bird catchers and the birds. These readers, particularly members of ethnic minorities and those who felt themselves socially handicapped, recognized certain elements of their own condition in the boy's struggle, and saw *The Painted Bird* as a reflection of their own struggle for intellectual, emotional or physical survival. They saw the boy's hardships in the marshes and forests continued in the ghettos and cities of another continent where color, language and education marked for life the "outsiders," the free-spirited wanderers whom the "insiders," the powerful majority, feared, ostracized and attacked. Still another group of readers approached the novel expecting it to expand their visions by admitting them into an otherworldly, Bosch-like landscape.

Today, years removed from the creation of *The Painted Bird*, I feel uncertain in its presence. The past decade has enabled me to regard the novel with a critic's detachment, but the controversy aroused by the book and the changes it caused in my own life and the lives of those close to me make me question my initial decision to write it.

I had not foreseen that the novel would take on a life of its own, that, instead of a literary challenge, it would become a threat to the lives of those close to me. To the rulers of my homeland, the novel, like the bird, had to be driven from the flock; having caught the bird, painted its feathers and released it, I simply stood by and watched as it wreaked its havoc. Had I foreseen what it would become, I might not have written *The Painted Bird*. But the book, like the boy, has weathered the assaults. The urge to survive is inherently unfettered. Can the imagination, any more than the boy, be held prisoner?

1976

NOTES OF THE AUTHOR ON THE PAINTED BIRD

Les images choisies par le souvenir sont aussi arbitraires, aussi étroites, aussi insaisissables, que celles que l'imagination avait formées et la réalité détruites. Il n'y a pas de raison pour qu'en dehors de nous un lieu réel possède plutôt les tableaux de la mémoire que ceux du rêve.

—MARCEL PROUST

The most essential stage of the writing process, it is often argued, is the process whereby the writer comes to stand outside the experience he intends to mirror in his book. The chief element of this "alienation" is the conscious desire to examine oneself and the experience from "without," from a standpoint at which both the writer himself and his surroundings lose their concrete features, and separate themselves from everyday reality after a long period of struggle and uncertainty to enter a fluid and less rigidly limited dimension. This new dimension exists only in the writer's consciousness; within it the elements of reality no longer obey the earthbound laws of gravitation; the minutiae of time and place cease to be important.

Between external reality and his own imagination the writer constructs one curtain after another. The number of these curtains and their effectiveness as filters for his thoughts are dictated by his temperament and creative vision. These curtains cannot completely veil reality; they merely obscure its patterns, reducing or magnifying its boundaries, accelerating or slowing its ceaseless movement.

As an actor playing Hamlet is neither Hamlet nor merely an actor, but, rather, an actor as Hamlet, so is a fictive event neither an actual event nor totally a created fiction with no base in experience; *it is an event as fiction.* A symbol is both concrete and abstract. It is neither literal reality nor illusion; it is both illusory and concrete. Naturally, the stimulus that gave birth to it can never be fully *known*; if it could, there would be no need for the symbol. It can never be defined; it can, at best, be interpreted. Marcel Proust stated this very clearly: "The grandeur of real art . . . is to rediscover, grasp again and lay before us that reality from which we live so far removed and from which we become more and more separated as the formal knowledge which we substitute for it grows in thickness and imperviousness—that reality which there is grave danger we might die without ever having known and yet which is simply our life."*

The transfer of fragments of objective reality to this new dimension in which the literary work arises has a logic of its own and requires the selection and condensation of a large number of phenomena which the writer believes to best document his imagination, best suit his adopted creative outlook. In this way, objective reality acquires for him a secondary importance; he makes use of it only to the extent to which it is already accommodated in the universe created by his imagination. *It might be said that the writer takes from outside himself only what he is capable of creating in his imagination.* "Imagination," writes Susanne K. Langer, "is probably the oldest mental trait that is typically human—older than discursive reason; it is probably the common source of dream, reason, religion, and all true general observation. It is this primitive human power—imagina-

* Marcel Proust, *The Vocation of the Artist,* in *The Creative Vision,* edited by Haskell M. Block and Herman Salinger, Grove Press. New York, 1960, pp. 78–79. For the original see: Marcel Proust, À *la Recherche du Temps Perdu,* Bibliothèque de la Pléiade, Librairie Gallimard, Paris, 1954, t. III, pp. 888–99.

tion—that engenders the arts and is in turn directly affected by their products."*

The artist's alienation from the specific experience seems to be an indispensable prerequisite for the creative process. Inevitably the book, in published form, will swoop back like a boomerang to that previous concrete life from which its writer had separated himself in order to create the book.

After the book is presented to the public, the writer becomes one of many readers of his own work, and his judgment of this work is yet another subjective judgment, neither more astute nor more shallow than the judgment of any other reader. "As for the *literal* interpretation," wrote Paul Valéry, "I have already set forth elsewhere my convictions on this subject; but it cannot be emphasized often enough; *there is no true meaning* of a text. The author has absolutely no authority. Whatever he may have *wanted to say*, he has written what he has written. Once published, a text is like a mechanism which everyone can use according to his ways and means: there is no certainty of its maker using it better than anyone else. Furthermore, if he really knows what he wanted to do, this knowledge always disturbs his perception of what he has done."† (Italics—Paul Valéry)

To say that *The Painted Bird* is nonfiction may be convenient for classification, but is not easily justified. Since our minds conceive of and empathize with created situations according to fixed patterns, certain fairly constant fictive realities (everything

*Susanne K. Langer, *Philosophical Sketches: A Study of the Human Mind in Relation to Feeling, Explored Through Art, Language, and Symbol*; New American Library: New York, 1964, p. 81.

†Paul Valéry, *Concerning Le Cimetière marin*, in *The Creative Vision*, op. cit. p. 39. For the original see: Paul Valéry, Préface, *Essai d'explication du "Cimetière marin."* Librairie Gallimard, Paris, 1933, pp. 7–33.

drawn from the depths of our memories, or dredged up from our subconscious levels of mind, or wrought from our creative abilities) will lack the hard edge of total fact. There are some obviously classic scenes in any culture—that is, in art, in literature and in the mind of an age: a child's reunion with lost parents, a lover's with a returning lover, death scenes, etc.— but these are not as subtle as the patterns we create unwittingly to help along our own thinking and identifying. These patterns are our individual little fictions. For we fit experiences into molds which simplify, shape and give them an acceptable emotional clarity. *The remembered event becomes a fiction, a structure made to accommodate certain feelings.* If there were not these structures, art would be too personal for the artist to create, much less for the audience to grasp. *There is no art which is reality; rather, art is the using of symbols by which an otherwise unstatable subjective reality is made manifest.* Even film, which is, of all the arts, the most capable of portraying the literal, is edited; if it were not, it would be either entirely incomprehensible or totally undigestible to the audience. This same editing process occurs in other art forms: remembering is the automatic process of editing. "Expression begins where thought ends," said Camus; this is creation; in this specific case, writing. Whether involved with nonfiction or fiction, the actively creating mind edits out what is unimportant or noncommunicable and directs itself toward the fictive situations. One cannot say that memory is either literal or exact; if memories have a truth, it is more an emotional than an actual one. It can be said that we transmute our experiences into little films. One example of the transformation of an experience into a mold for an emotion, where the work is classified as nonfiction, although not accurately, is Albert Camus' essay *Return to Tipasa.* When Camus wrote of his return to the North African town of Tipasa, he certainly was writing of the actual Tipasa as a symbol. Certainly, also, he had visited Tipasa, had once lived there and was then revisiting the town. But the actual visit, although it was important as the particular choice of a situation in which to encase specific emotions, was subordinate to those specific emotions which he *may have felt* in Tipasa, but which he wished to convey to his reader. Also, this particular selection of symbolic setting further directs the reader to sensory identification, by the selection of detail within the selection of setting; this process, if not unconscious, is at least partially spontaneous and directs the senses to the emotional level in which the work's specific emotional truths will be most strongly revealed. The essay, one presumes, is autobiographical: Albert Camus, troubled, returns to a place with which he had always associated peace and lucidity and the serenity of nature; he walks along the beach and finds that in the middle of winter he has within himself an invincible summer. But even this discovery must be expressed in symbols, forming a situation in which the literal and the symbolic approach one another so closely that from the confrontation arises the meaning.

In order to produce the image of remembering, the author organized *The Painted Bird* in little dramas, in spurts of experience, with the links largely omitted, as is the case with memory. The extremity of the situations, through heightened action and imagery, reproduces also the action of our thoughts and our dreams. The symbolic quality of the characters and details of the situation are also valid, since, in remembering, dreaming or creating fiction, each serves as a method of conserving and underlining something else, as a concretization of a feeling. But, one could ask, why was this book written about childhood? Why did the author choose this particular motif? C. G. Jung, in his essay *The Psychology of the Child Archetype*, provides enlightening viewpoints. Jung regards the child motif as representative of the preconscious state of human consciousness, the childhood of the mental processes, of which traces still remain in all of us; this he terms "the Collective Unconscious." He writes: ". . . the analogy of certain psychological experiences . . . [shows] . . . that certain phases of an individual's life can become autonomous, can personify themselves to the extent that they result in a vision of oneself—for instance, one sees oneself as a child. Visionary experiences of this kind, whether in dreams or in the waking state, are, as we know, conditional on a dissociation having previously taken place between past and present. Such dissociations come about because of various incapabilities; for instance, a man's present state may have come into conflict with his childhood state, or he may have violently sundered himself from his original character in the interests of some arbitrary *persona* more in keeping with his ambitions . . . He has thus become childlike and artificial, and he has lost his roots. All this presents a favorable opportunity of an equally vehement confrontation with the primary truth."*

The Painted Bird, then, could be the author's vision of himself as a child, a *vision*, not an examination, or a revisitation of childhood. This vision, this search for something lost, can only be conducted in the metaphor through which the unconscious most easily manifests itself, and toward which the unconscious most naturally navigates. The locale and the setting are likewise metaphorical, for the whole journey could actually have taken place in the mind. Just as the setting is metaphorical, so do the characters become archetypes, symbols of things equally felt and equally intangible—the symbols, though, being doubly real, since they are the expression of the things they represent.

Possibly the book defies immediate and simple classification.

*C. G. Jung and C. Kerényi, *Essays on a Science of Mythology*, Harper & Row, New York, 1963; translated by R.F.C. Hull, pp. 80–81. For the original see: C. G. Jung and C. Kerényi, *Einführung in das Wesen der Mythologie*, Zurich, 1941 (Part II: The Psychology of the Child Archetype, #1. The Archetype as a Link with the Past).

The names used in *The Painted Bird* are fictional and cannot with any justification whatsoever be ascribed to any particular national group. The area is only vaguely defined, since the border regions, continually torn by strife, had no unity of nationality or faith. Thus no ethnic or religious group has cause to believe itself to be represented, and no chauvinistic feelings need be set on edge. Just as the cemetery makes anonymous the lives of those that lie beneath, so have time and political change rendered unrecognizable the distinguishing features of life in the area where this story unfolds.

The content of the book presents problems. Expanded fact is not fiction; enriched memory is not simple invention. To the publisher the area between is traditionally no-man's-land. In his work *Aesthetic Relation of Art to Reality*, N. G. Chernyshevsky wrote in 1855 that ". . . no matter how good a memory one may have, it cannot retain all the details, especially those that are unimportant for the essence of the event; but many of them are needed for the artistic completeness of the story and must be borrowed from other scenes . . . True, the addition of these details does not alter the event and, so far, the difference between the artistic narrative and the event related in it is only one of form. But the intervention of the imagination is not limited to this. In reality, the event overlapped other events only outwardly connected with it, there was no inherent connection between them. When we separate the event we have chosen from the other events and from the unnecessary episodes, we find that this operation leaves new gaps in the living fullness of the story . . ." *

Fact and memory: Is the book simply the product of these two faculties? *The Painted Bird* is rather the result of the slow

---

*N. G. Chernyshevsky, *Aesthetic Relation of Art to Reality*, in N. G. Chernyshevsky, *Selected Philosophical Essays*, Foreign Languages Publishing House, Moscow, 1953, p. 377.

unfreezing of a mind long gripped by fear, of isolated facts that have become interwoven into a tapestry. The light of memory is less brilliant, but the illumination spreads to a broader area, and is softer, more sympathetic. Foregrounds lose in definition, and backgrounds emerge from the shadows. Those formerly remembered only for their acts can now be assessed for their characters. Events to the child are immediate: discoveries are one-dimensional. This kills, that maims, this one cuffs, that one caresses. But to the adult the vision of these memories is multidimensional. Hunger is no longer an intermittent memory as it was then, fear is no longer an irregular pulse as it once was. These are no longer absorbed by the body as the changing fortunes of the passing days. Rather they appear now to have been the seams and bindings of a way of life.

Superstition and fear, watching plague and waiting death, sunless forest and frozen marsh, the iron fetters of hunger that bind the wearied peasant to the unyielding soil, the suspicions that turn him from his neighbor, the fears that unite him against the stranger, the knowledge of joylessness, the expectation of disaster. The grudged devotion to an unforgiving God, the persistent fear of the nearer portents borne by bird and beast, the unrelenting hunt of ghoul and ghost for the human soul, the many snares for the unwary. These forces cannot be bound within neat, divided, categorized notes. Marta, Stupid Ludmila, Laba and Makar are people of their villages, and have no existence outside the village. The anthropologist could no more pin the facts of their lives to the printed page than he could those of the witches in *Macbeth*.

The events have lost their isolation, have merged and fluxed, ebbed and flowed through the author's mind like tides. He gives the cloth of his experience, not merely threads. The threads are woven, and the resulting patterns are more than the threads, but their colors and textures are still wholly valid. He draws up not simply an adult's catalogue of tidy facts, but spills out the involved, pain-racked, fear-heightened memories, impressions and feelings of the child. He cannot set a precise measure around all this. He gives not the record of an escape, but the experiences of a part of a human life, of a fugitive who greeted each dawn with mixed feelings, who fears more than welcomes each new day, who sees not the promise of sun, but feels the threat of storm.

"It is a striking paradox in all child myths," writes Jung, "that the 'child' is on the one hand delivered helpless into the power of terrible enemies and in continual danger of extinction, while on the other he possesses powers far exceeding those of ordinary humanity."* In the book the child (the Boy) survives because he cannot do otherwise, because he is a total incarnation of the urge for self-realization and self-preservation. He possesses no ability to limit himself, or to prevent the full force of his potential from developing. Rather he is equipped only with those powers of nature and instinct which further his ability to survive. The conscious mind is halted and tied up by its inability *to do otherwise*; 'the child,' therefore, resists to the utmost any threat, however small, to his safety. To prove this, he is put to test after test. It can be seen that every such test described in the book employs palpable natural symbols—fire, water, mud and excrement; he is buried; he is cast alone into the wilderness. Yet he must survive. The fact that the narrative is written in the first person implies certainty that he will. The choosing of the child as conductor of the search can be especially enlightening, since only in the growth of the child can we observe an approximation of the mind's evolutionary processes. The child perceives through and learns from the same symbols as did the prehistoric tribes—for example, animal imagery and instinctual

---

*C. G. Jung and C. Kerényi, *Essays on a Science of Mythology*. Part III: The Special Phenomenology of the Child Archetype: #2. The Invincibility of the Child; *Op. cit..* p. 89.

association with the natural. Here again, the preoccupation with speech and lack of it is interesting. The Boy cannot speak the dialect of the region, and then, when he is beginning to be able to, he is deprived of the power of speech entirely. Obviously, the author purposefully prevents the Boy from having the advantage of normal communication. This imposed silence fulfills several functions.

When the means of speech is lost to him, the Boy is consequently thrown back onto motivated action. Whereas speech may be a substitute for action, or an oblique method of suggesting it, action speaks for itself.

The modern literary use of language is contrapuntal, employed to lay bare the significant area which exists between language and action, and to highlight the gulf between them. This gulf also seems to be the focal point of modern art. But in *The Painted Bird* the situation is taken further; in the attempt to recall the primitive, the symbols are sought more pertinently and immediately than through the superficial process of speech and dialogue. In addition, the sense of alienation is heightened by depriving the characters of the ability to communicate freely. Observation is a silent process; without the means of participation, the silent one must observe. Perhaps this silence is also a metaphor for dissociation from the community and from something greater. This feeling of alienation floats on the surface of the work and manifests the author's awareness, perhaps unconscious, of his break with the wholeness of self.

In *The Painted Bird* one textual device frequently employed is the use of a natural subplot. Human action is either first enacted or subsequently repeated in animal images. A forceful example is the dinner scene at the miller's, when the two cats are used to evoke the heightened air of sexual tension which exists, but

exists mainly as an undercurrent. In fact, this device is doubly
used, since it is introduced into the action by the miller to
achieve the same effect the author wishes to produce on the
reader. This double use of image and underscoring results in a
richer, more revealing narrative. This device is employed several
times by the author, most fully when the coital seizure of dogs
provides an expanded parallel to the situation of Rainbow and
the Jewish girl. A third use of this device is the continued
statement of image, its prolonged use throughout the narrative,
culminating in its metamorphosis into a symbol. A prime example of this is the image of the painted bird. Finally, there is the
unstated behavioral and psychological analogy between character and animal: the Jews on the train, the girl whom Rainbow
rapes, the boy dying by the tracks, the babies hurled from the
moving cars, all form a striking parallel with the flayed rabbit
dazedly running around the yard. The rats' attack on the carpen-
ter in the bunker parallels the Kalmuks' attack on the village.
Then, too, each character's most real image is an animal: Garbos
and the wolfhound, Lekh and the painted birds; the continual
identification with the animal as the outsider—the pigeon at
Marta's hut, the painted birds at Lekh's cabin, all these point
toward the dominant image of the Boy. Another use of the
natural is in the juxtaposition of life and death: the extermination camp trains run past the villages most frequently during
the fecund days of the mushroom harvest; the community's
severest action against the Boy takes place on Corpus Christi
Day and, significantly, in a churchyard; a murder is committed
during a wedding feast, which is thus turned into a funeral
gathering. The peasants ghoulishly loot the bodies of dead Jews,
carrying the souvenirs home in great triumph—a photograph of
a murdered Jew hangs next to a religious picture. Familiar fictive
structures are employed and totally inverted: the wanderings of
the Silent One and the Boy comprise an idyll of childhood,

completely blackened by the tragedy of their situation. The reconciliation scene with the parents is likewise inverted: indifference replaces joy. Lekh and Ludmila, one mad, the other demented, are the inamorati of a story in which hate is a dominant emotion.

Thus *The Painted Bird* strips reality down to natural terms, insinuating clues to a metaphysical frame in order to construct a morality. It is an attempt to peel the gloss off the world, to view life without the comfortable conceits with which we embellish perceptible reality. Such a search leads back to the metaphor of childhood, with a resultant prevalence of natural images and motifs—dreams, phallic symbols, the images we have learned to associate with fairy tales. With the gilt and crimson façade gone, the black roots of the fairy tale manifest themselves. *The Painted Bird* can be considered as fairy tales *experienced* by the child, rather than *told* to him: the SS become those slightly more than human heroes who perform deeds of incredible difficulty with incredible ease; Ludmila is the maiden of the woods; the invincible weapons become the comet, the gun and "soap"; there are witches, trolls, terrible forests and great searches. These are all devices by which the search back to the primitive is achieved. Again, the roots of the unconscious are tapped. There are, in all of us, mainstreams of psychological effect which cannot fail to produce this reaction. Their power to rouse us is inherent and actual, and our shock at the incidents in *The Painted Bird* may well be one of recognition. And perhaps this recognition is of the self, a self with which we are either entirely unfamiliar or of which we are only faintly aware through the content of our dreams and fantasies: "The symbols of self," says Jung, "arise in the depths of the body and they express its materiality every bit as much as the structure of the perceiving consciousness. The symbol is thus a living body, *Corpus et Anima*; hence, the 'child' is such an apt formula for the symbol."*

2
1
3

The world depicted in *The Painted Bird* may be regarded as a world of distinctive elementary symbols, simple keys to the European culture of the mid-twentieth century. Today, twenty-five years later, many of these symbols still remain unrecognized. For like the peasants collecting photographs thrown out of "death trains," we similarly find in the daily newspapers endless descriptions and photographs of atrocities committed somewhere, by someone, to someone. And, like those peasants, the passive onlookers at the grand spectacle of violence and destruction, we, hiding in the privacy of our comfortable homes, watch television programs. Day after day, evening after evening, the images and sounds of human tragedies occurring *elsewhere* leap onto the screens: falling bombs, collapsing houses, people being murdered or tortured because of their origin, faith, opinions, color of skin. No disaster goes unnoticed. In our eyes, as in the eyes of Lekh the bird catcher, innocent victims go down each day, like the painted birds loosed only to be killed by others because their coloring differed. And meanwhile we look at these spectacles in the calm awareness that all these cruelties and crimes are happening *elsewhere*, far away, and being committed by *others* who must have their own reasons for acting thus, while we ourselves, though disturbed and outraged, have nothing to do with it—and indeed, we do not want to have anything to do with any of it. In *Incident at Vichy* Arthur Miller stated it in this way:

LEDUC: I owe you the truth, Prince; you won't believe it now, but I wish you would think about it and what it means. I have never analyzed a gentile who did not have, somewhere hidden in his mind, a dislike if not a hatred for the Jews.

* *Ibidem*, p. 92

TIME   OF   LIFE,   TIME   OF   ART

VON BERG: That is impossible, it is not true of me!

LEDUC: Until you know it is true of you you will destroy whatever truth can come out of this atrocity. Part of knowing who you are is knowing we are not someone else. And Jew is only the name we give to that stranger, that agony we cannot feel, that death we look at like a cold abstraction. Each man has his Jew; it is the other. And the Jews have their Jews. And now, now above all, you must see that you have yours—the man whose death leaves you relieved that you are not him, despite your decency. And that is why there is nothing and will be nothing—until you face your own complicity with this . . . your own humanity.*

We are astonished by the cruelty and primitiveness of the peasants in this book. Is it possible, we ask, for people to be so harsh as not to protect a small defenseless boy? How can they look unfeelingly at trains carrying thousands of people to a horrible death? How can they torture a victim who has succeeded in escaping? Let us dwell on this for an instant. These peasants endured in ignorance and in cruelty, but the important thing is that they did endure. And this is the case with human society as a whole; the peasantlike mentality of self-protection and survival exceeds all national borders. The history of mankind is the history of such an endurance. Plagues have killed millions and wars have drained off enormous quantities of lives, but qualitatively, life goes on.

The lessons learned from the Boy's wanderings, even if they provide no absolute answers, do underline and affirm the peasants' ability to challenge an external pressure and, whenever they can, to seek out and to take advantage of the similarities between their own mentality and that of the oppressors. Thus justification is brought into the battle against the deadly threats

* Arthur Miller, *Incident at Vichy*, Viking Press, New York, 1965, p. 66.

of the occupation. If their survival was partly due to the persecution of some within their own numbers because of gratuitous
agreement in doctrine with their enemies, so much the better.
The peasants achieved at least their own survival.

Were the peasants of *The Painted Bird* more cruel than their
not too distant neighbors? Did not the trains carrying people to
their final destiny come directly from that "civilized" world of
modern cities filled with the relics of a thousand years of culture,
with their electricity, broadcasting stations, hospitals, schools,
libraries, and learned societies? Could these peasants suddenly
forget what the ubiquitous *Bekanntmachungen* (notices) perpetu-
ally reminded them about: that the penalty was death for giving
shelter or aid to any Jew or Gypsy *under any circumstances whatsoever.* This law was not conceived in the remote poverty-stricken
villages of Eastern Europe. The peasants did not write this law;
it came to them expressly from that "civilized" world and was
carried to them on the bayonets of the army of occupation. Its
writing and promulgation were undertaken by men educated in
the centers of European culture, brought up with knowledge of
the Renaissance and Enlightenment, of the philosophy of Kant,
Hegel and Schopenhauer, loving the music of Bach, Beethoven
and Mozart, the poetry of Goethe and Schiller, and aware of
the prose of the finest minds of their generation.

This law was introduced into their lives by the engineers and
technicians of Death; not only in the villages of Eastern Europe,
but also throughout all of Nazi-occupied Europe it tolerated no
exceptions and had no loopholes. Could a small fugitive boy,
with his dangerous resemblance to a Jew or Gypsy, find any safe
place in occupied Europe during the war?

This war was not started by the peasants. Like millions of
educated and "civilized" city dwellers, they became its victims.
Throughout this war the peasants of Eastern Europe were not
relics of the past, an underdeveloped society missed by the
progress of civilization. On the contrary, the peasants in *The*

Painted Bird symbolize and personify the level to which the so-called European civilization was forced down by World War II. These peasants became part of the great holocaust of violence, murder, lawlessness and destruction which the war had been preparing for them. They understood this terror, because it occurred within the elementary categories of brutality, committed by the strong against the weak, by the victor over the vanquished, by the armed over the unarmed. If they were not surprised by individual scenes in this cataclysm and if they even occasionally took part in it, it was precisely because this happening proceeded at their level and they required no "education" or "civilization" for it. They were not surprised by the persecution of Jews and Gypsies, since they were taught by their fathers—who in turn had been taught by theirs—that Jews deserved no pity because they had killed the Son of God and hence, by the virtue of this very fact, God himself is hostile to them and is preparing for them a terrible though just punishment. From time immemorial the peasants had known that those murderers of the Son of God could be recognized by their black hair, black eyes, hooked noses, olive skins, and circumcized members. And that is how the theories of racism, of the "scientifically proven" necessity of genocide, became so easily accepted by some simple, uneducated peasants in the rural fastnesses of Eastern Europe.

At the same time, as we must not forget, the peasants in *The Painted Bird* are not simply cruel because they desire to be cruel and delight in this emotion. Their cruelty is extremely defensive, elemental, sanctioned by traditions, by faith and superstition, by centuries of poverty, exploitation, disease, and by the ceaseless depredations of stronger neighbors. What Antonin Artaud wrote about cruelty fully applies to these peasants: "In the practice of cruelty there is a kind of higher determinism, to which the executioner-tormentor himself is subjected and which he must be determined to endure when the time comes.

Cruelty is above all lucid, a kind of rigid control and submission to necessity."* This cruelty is borne out in the characters of the peasants. Though they may not fall within the anthropological definition of "primitive," their lives are certainly more closely bound up with age-old tribally based traditions than are the fragmented existences of urbanites in more developed areas. The peasants have not been so severed from the oneness of the primitive mentality, and they stand without dissent within the restraints of tradition and superstition, the comforting blanket under which a people feel a unifying interdependence. Perhaps their "perversions," their individual deviations, appear either as perfectly natural, or as compulsions cast upon them by an external force. They are not consciously aware of having willed their acts. These compulsions arise and are carried out. "If our life lacks a brimstone, i.e., a constant magic, it is because we choose to observe our acts and lose ourselves in considerations of their imagined form instead of being impelled by their force,"† to quote again Antonin Artaud. This statement, uttered in the course of a plea to society to return to the primitive cultural standard, applies perfectly to the peasants of the book: to Lekh, Garbos, Ewka, Makar and the others. Their acts are governed by their instincts. Although they are far from leading a prehistoric existence, they have remained rather primitive in their psychological evolution.

Into their midst wanders the myth-figure, the fugitive Boy. He is the living incarnation of a motif with which their collective unconscious still has affinity, a symbol which is still highly potent, although not specifically or formally identifiable. He is a child whose existence can lay bare their spirits in terrible and

---

*Antonin Artaud, *The Theater and Its Double*, Grove Press, New York, 1958; translated by Mary C. Richards, p. 102. For the original see: Antonin Artaud, *Le Théâtre et son Double*, Lettre 1e, Gallimard, Collection Métamorphoses, No. IV, 1938.

†Antonin Artaud, *The Theater and Its Double*, Preface, *Op cit.* p. 8.

wonderful ways: he provokes their passions; he causes them to fall back onto their deepest instincts; he brings them into contact with that public and private past which stirs up the settledness and threatens the security of their involved ignorances. The Boy comes into their isolated world at the same time as the Germans, a very real threat of annihilation, arrive. The peasants, caught in the midst of this process, already aroused by the war, are worked up, compelled to violent action by the pressures of these many tensions rising to the surface. But, it seems, there is another side to these feelings. There is an instinct that lies behind the fear and that makes these peasants consider the child as one who must not be destroyed. Perhaps in their deepest thoughts lies the belief that while both the arrival and the appearance of the Boy endanger them, yet he *may* have been sent to save. Two embodiments of some inexplicable feeling simultaneously coexist and are in conflict. Their actual occurrence together (the Boy in church, serving at the Mass), brings the peasants' many contradictory emotions into turmoil, and the former's apparent invalidation of the latter opened emotional floodgates when the Boy ominously let fall the missal during Mass. It is also noteworthy that a community threatened with destruction or with a breakup of its cultural forms clings with renewed ferocity to the mythic; the stresses of war produce this group reaction, bringing added tension into both the communal and the individual consciousnesses.

It seems, therefore, that all the adults in this book are positive heroes, because they did not kill the Boy. During a period when a human life often was not worth the bullet with which it could be taken, the fact that a solitary boy, thought to be a Jew or a Gypsy, did survive the war is undoubtedly remarkable. Hundreds of thousands of children died in the ghettos, in the bombed cities, in the concentration camps. They died from hunger, disease or violence. Hundreds of thousands of others were crippled for life. The adults in this book, however, contributed to the survival of the Boy during the war, when he was among strangers whom death threatened for sheltering or aiding him in any way. Others—the Germans—had the military duty of killing any unaccounted-for persons. They, too, risked their lives if they failed in their duties.

So much about positive heroism. This book has, however, also a negative hero.

He is the Boy.

Of all the characters he alone hates consciously, continuously, and most deeply; he desires and thirsts to hate others for all that had happened to him in this world. Everyday life provides him both with this hatred and with many possibilities for expressing it. In this respect, *The Painted Bird* provides an example of the formation of a unique destructive drive in which even the mechanisms become agents of destruction, and those who control them gain power through their possession (the comet, "soap," etc.). Mitka the Cuckoo's rifle is a palpable instance of this symbolic relationship.

The most unlikely things become involved in the development of this consuming force. Trains, for example, play a vital role in this process and are the vehicles through which two highly significant episodes are carried to their conclusion. The first has to do with camp-bound trains carrying Jews to their deaths, and in the second a score of innocent peasants meet with death under very different circumstances when the Silent One derails a market-bound train as his revenge for a humiliation. In the first of these two cases the trains offer an additional challenge to the Boy. His greatest pleasure comes from the nerve-racking, danger-fraught sport of lying between the tracks while the trains speed over him. He exposes himself to and survives the danger that the trains present. In the second case, that of the market-bound train, the oppressed become the oppressors. Those who might have been borne away to the camps by the trains are now destroying the peasants who stood by as the trains roared past. It is those who were so nearly victims who now stand by the tracks and silently rejoice. Hate can be a machine as functional and regular as a locomotive; it will always pass by, and there will always be some people cheering as it passes, silently or not. The Boy finally emerged from the world of the concentration camp trains and the hostile peasants, but he emerged knowing he would never be entirely free from it. He is returned to his parents wiser on account of what he has learned in his wanderings, but his wisdom has a horrifying quality. Yet it is only by employing its lessons of hate and revenge that he is able to part himself from it. This hate allows him to see with some clarity why and what he hates. Paradoxically this process causes his desires for revenge and his capacity for hatred to cease being directed at *any single person or group*; now they become attitudes, deeply ingrained, the wellspring of the purpose of his life, the basis for his behavior *in all situations*. The Boy is thus back exactly where he started and as alone as when he was removed from his parents. The wanderer becomes a stranger again, and his "suprapersonal" philosophy can be redirected, reoriented (if help is needed, through an indoctrination process, for example), and can be refocused on other specific persons or groups or systems of thought. So the survivors are eager *to remember*, more than ready *to avenge*. And people need so little stimulation to hate again and again. There will always be another train. Who, then, is guilty? The people who pull the switch, or those who stand by the tracks and cheer? Both? Which one? Neither? In any case, the modern examples of mass destruction are examples of a mechanism's potential being gloriously realized by a human mechanism.

This modern hate, this particular genre of revenge, can be a very solitary thing—perhaps "solitary" is not the correct word; perhaps "individual" is better. Maybe hate is a way of self-fulfillment? For hate takes on a mystical aura; to possess hate is to possess great power, and the wielder of that power has control of magnificent gifts. Like Prospero he rules his kingdom, and justice is meted out according to his will. Things are as he sees them to be; if not, they soon submit to his vision of the world. He can shape his world as he wills: Prospero's wand becomes revenge.

If this implies a total disregard for the objectively real, a marvelously one-sided and incomplete view, it is all the more honest for this. Who can set a price on the crimes committed against the Boy by the peasants? Certainly not a bystander, who has experienced nothing. Certainly not the peasants, who acted without consciousness of the experience. The Boy himself is the only one capable of knowing the quality of the act, of judging the offense and of deciding on the penalty.

Unlike Vendice in Cyril Tourneur's *The Revenger's Tragedy*, one doesn't need to face the victim; there is no demand for him to recognize the agent of his destruction. That was a melodramatic gesture made for the audience's benefit. Now it is the *act* of revenge, that counts, the *act* above all. Mitka the Cuckoo, the heroic Soviet sniper, needs only to kill; in the performance of the act he has avenged the wrongs committed against him and he can live with his own sense of himself reaffirmed. He has never hesitated to take responsibility for his actions; he accepted it all along. And so the Boy survives the war, filled with the terrible poison of hatred which gives him a goal to live for and therefore helps him to endure. From a defenseless victim in the hands of pursuers he becomes a living symbol of those who had previously pursued him. Pity is alien to him. He does not believe in the charismatic power of religion. He feels himself to be betrayed and deceived; he carries within himself his own brand of justice and metes out punishment to others according to his own reckoning. To him the world is merely a forgotten bunker where the rats murder one another without hope of escape. For

2
2
2

this world he feels only boundless contempt and hate; and the shadow of this contempt will lengthen as the Boy grows. . . .

The Boy in *The Painted Bird* embodies the drama of our culture: the tragedy of the crime always remains with the living. This drama cannot be killed on the fronts, bombed in cities, confined in concentration camps. This drama is borne by all the survivors of the crime, both the conquerors and the conquered. Its essence is hate.

The victors are convinced of the effectiveness and justice of this hate by the fact that they succeeded in vanquishing the hated enemy. The vanquished see their hatred confirmed by having suffered defeat at the hands of a hated victor. Both refer to those who "gave their life for the cause, for the homeland, for justice." Both desire only once more, for the last time, to pay the sacred blood debt of revenge. Both, like the peasants in *The Painted Bird*, oppose the final cleansing of the bloodstains from the place of the killings. Both bring children to see these bloodstains; the children who survived the Holocaust and still feel dread, pain and humiliation, who remember hunger, the noise of bombs and the cries of the innocent who were dragged away. Both victor and vanquished point out these bloodstains to the young and whisper tautly: do you remember your murdered uncle, grandfather, father, mother? Know that you may not forget, because, my little one, on you depends the solemn cause of avenging them and carrying forward for us, who are old and tired, the fiercely burning torch of sacred vengeance. . . .

And the children, the painted birds themselves, gaze at the bloodstains—in order to remember.

Thus no death is granted to hate: virulent and as vital as life itself, it follows in the wake of life, and as the tail is part of the comet, so is hate a part of life itself.

1965

THE ART OF THE SELF:
ESSAYS
À PROPOS *STEPS*

O what a mask was there, what a disguise!
—MILTON

He who is really living
exists as if being dead.
—GUNNAR EKELOFF

S*teps** has no plot in the sense of Aristotelian tragedy in which characters must be, as legendary figures always have been, "true to tradition." In Aristotle's terms for the revelation of the action, the end fulfills the beginning and the middle determines the end. But the aim of *Steps* precludes such an ordering of time. The relationship of the characters exists in the fissure between past and present. And it is precisely between the past and present of the incidents of *Steps* that the projected struggle takes place. The incidents are interludes in the contest, and, as in Greek drama, they are the vehicle of its lyric and thematic sense: the incident is the symbol, the enactment of the struggle. "My stress lay on the incidents in the development of a soul; little else is worth study": in these words of Browning one could sum up the stress laid upon the reader by the neither horizontal nor vertical narrative staircase of *Steps*.

Given the reader's experiences (in daily life they constitute the reader's armor in any encounter with a stranger), the reader may perceive the work in a form of his own devising, automati-

* *Steps*, a novel by Jerzy Kosinski, Random House, 1968, won the 1969 National Book Award in Fiction.

cally filling in its intentionally loose construction with his own formulated experiences, fantasies and storytelling vertigo. The reader's gain in each incident of *Steps* is the result of his own sifting through and refining of much of the novel's imagery. The reader leaves each episode with a hint of recognition, an intimation—no more. This reception runs counter to that of the conventional contemporary melodrama which gains its effects from predetermined emotional group responses.

Steps is the log of an odyssey in which action, memory and emotion unite to captivate the mind and compel the reader (the spectator, the hearer) to feel the need to read on. The reader's need to read on, to move from one page to the next (or even to return to an incident as one does to one's neighbor next door) corresponds to the narrator's urge to pursue one experience (self-exposure) after another.

From the reader's viewpoint *Steps* offers a multiple choice. Such a tactic is subversive: if the reader accepts this offer and follows the narrator, he may be trapped. The narrative suggests a carefully designed pace; the details of the story are intricately yet symmetrically arranged, luring the reader deeper into the book while retarding the disturbing aura of conflict.

At the end of every consecutive incident *Steps* allows the reader to break his journey—or to continue reading. In the fissure separating these possibilities, the *agon*, the struggle between the book (the predator) and the reader (the victim), takes place.

The beginning of *Steps*: "I was traveling farther south," creates the opening for the reader's entry into the book; as it now opens, the reader immediately becomes the wanderer. His own wisdom might lead him to suspect that in an age of limited and fixed purposes, iconoclasm could well be the last gesture available before indifference.

In classical French drama, scenes are marked by the exit or entrance of a character. In *Steps* the episode is also most clearly demarcated. With each new exit or entrance there is a development of the point of view; consecutive actions are introduced and completed; meanings already hinted at are discarded or added to. In contemporary thought and contemporary artistic forms, the demarcations are not so sharp, and the editing is more subjective: witness the *roman-fleuve*. It is no longer felt that meaning lies only in incident following incident; we now recognize the importance of pattern.

Episodes display their symbolism when worked into *montage*, through which they establish patterns, while preserving the memory of a master symbol.

Montage reflects the modern thought process. Thus, for instance, psychoanalysis is a means of creating a *montage*. The cinematic image has become the key to modern perception. It has created a new relationship between visual perception and emotion.

We seem to perceive reality in episodes, in groups of organized "acknowledgments." The episode—in its extension, the plot—is the objective correlative of the work, the way meaning is conveyed to the reader. What lies between episodes is both a comment on and something commented upon by the episode. Episodes in the memory embody and guide the less concrete, the more encapsulated of our thoughts.

Modern art attempts to break down the blocks of perceptions in order to create a reality of pure perception, reality before it is formed into episodes. It objects to the imposing on the present a form of the past, since it claims that original perception precedes all forms.

Loneliness is facing oneself. Everything and the only thing that the protagonist of *Steps* is aware of is his self, and that is ephemeral. He knows himself by hints, by allusions; he approaches himself and steps away from himself; he looks for himself in others, hoping that every new situation would bring forth a new "I."

Thus, he seeks unforeseen situations to take the place of his predictable imagination; this signifies no moral judgment that accompanies these many preferences. He acts with full comprehension of his own awareness; hence he is anti-acting in the sense that he creates each situation rather than being a reactor in it.

The leitmotif of *Steps* is metamorphosis. The protagonist changes his external appearance and plays all the characters. He is a tourist, archaeological assistant, skiing instructor, a deserting soldier, a sniper in the army, a photographer. His metamorphosis follows his design even when it is involuntary. Alternating, he remembers himself as a child during the war, as a student at the university, as a lecturer on a collective farm. His entrance often leads to the metamorphosis of others: the credit card in the first incident of the novel becomes the magical object which transforms and releases the peasant girl from herself. The protagonist's girlfriend is raped at the party given by his friends. A haughty office girl is required to subject herself to the "whim of the man she loved" and subsequently allows herself to be possessed at his command by the narrator, whom she is never permitted to see.

By the outcome, the priority of reality over imagination is

established throughout *Steps*, and for the narrator reality becomes a prerequisite of consciousness of self.

In the light of the modern understanding of perception and
consciousness, the forms of art based on a conception of time as
objective and chronological (in which all events are of equal
importance because they follow a real temporal sequence which
exists outside the individual consciousness) may no longer apply.

Now we try to show time as we perceive it, and show experience as we absorb it. The shaping mind is at the center of the
work and guides the work as it evolves. The work is the point
of view.

Taking the visual for its theme "op art" causes us to perceive
the nature of perception and makes us conscious of how we
perceive.

Steps is written in intentionally nonfigurative language since its
narrator censors and suppresses any act stemming from his
imagination. Nevertheless, in the incident of the narrator's
involvement with the tubercular woman, he is not able to preserve the autonomy of reality similar to that of the autonomy of
his imagination. ". . . I concentrated more and more on the
thought that it was I who stood there in the mirror and that it
was my flesh her hands and lips were touching."

Through the use of language, the protagonist cannot prevent
his imagination interfering with reality. Such interference takes
place when a hospital nun, as if announcing a verdict, accuses
him of being a hyena who feeds upon the dying woman. And
though he is standing in the midst of a landscape of snow-
covered valleys and hills, instantly and inescapably her words
evoke in him the vision of a drought-stricken plain. Later in the
story, as if fearful of such interference, the protagonist discards

language altogether and surrenders to voluntary mutism. The abandonment of linguistic expression signifies his desire to rely on the power of gesture; his destiny is thus *made* and not *expressed*. This secession from language performs a further function in *Steps*: it increases the moral ambiguity of the work in which the reality is always manipulated and seldom judged.

Set in italics in order to separate them from the rest of the narrative, the passages of dialogue within the novel abbreviate and articulate the action, insinuating visual and emotive activity. These fragments of conversations may be viewed simply as one more example of the protagonist's past, as his recall of verbalized intimacies. Or they may be considered another self's reactions to what the narrator (or, indeed, the author) said in the book. In either case they indicate why the narrator-memoirist selects certain incidents from his life, and what impact he expects to achieve—or has already achieved—as a result of telling his story.

While we certainly do not know strangers better than we know those with whom we are intimate, we do know strangers in more neatly defined terms. We see strangers as blocks of objective traits identified with what lies in our past. We see them in theatrical terms; the complexity of mutual identification still lies ahead, since we are not yet involved; we respond to them now as to characters in the early scenes of a play. We are still discovering; we are not empathizing. Not yet. The barrier between the illusory and the real, between sympathy and empathy, is still definite. At this point, we have not yet begun to care.

From the viewpoint of the protagonist of *Steps*, the only truly satisfying relationship is one growing out of domination, one in which his experience—a certain form of the past—can be projected onto the other person. Until this hold is gained (assuming that the "prey" has some awareness of the protagonist's purpose), the "prey" maintains some superiority over the protagonist and remains his rival.

The narrator of *Steps* installs electronic listening devices in the apartments of strangers and monitors their voices. After a while he establishes an intimate relationship with one of the strangers, a woman whose life has thus become familiar to him. And so, without her knowledge, he has absorbed something essentially hers, her own past.

If there is anything in a person which enables that person to remain independent, the protagonist of *Steps* attempts to conquer that independence; if he succeeds he feels only indifference. But in a seemingly prolonged moment when the dominance becomes his, he feels a kind of passion, a gratefulness so total, a joy at winning so deep as to be love. There grows within him also great relief at having finally freed himself of a struggle, of finally being able to acknowledge himself the stronger. In that instant when one partner loves the other's susceptibility, he loves passionately.

But when that instant passes, he feels only emptiness and he moves again from threat to conquest, from love to indifference. The issue of solipsism is always at the center of such dark art—and the game of expropriation is always momentary and hence illusory.

When the narrator has become so intimately involved with this woman that he succeeds in unburdening himself by means of grafting his past onto her, when the relationship no longer has any valid function, then he no longer needs her, since the forms of his past and his effort to discard them were the basis of his need.

Not only is the woman no longer needed, she is also no longer wanted. She is now his past, and that he has discarded. It was a necessary act because his past was crippling him, preventing him from acting fully in the present. The narrator's projections serve also an opposite function: that of a mutual shield thrust out to prevent the admission of the present and to perpetuate and intensify shared memories. The hostility discernible in his relationships indicates an occasional recognition of the deception, of the fact that they serve solely as a defense: defense against spontaneity. Defense against being dominated by the present moment.

If sin is any act which prevents the self from functioning freely, the greatest sources of sin are those formerly protective agencies like society and religion. The original sense of "creative" becomes completely reversed; now the only possible creative act, the independent act of choice and self-enhancement, seems to be the destructive act—as in Sade. In *Crime and Punishment* Raskolnikov kills for the sake of independence, and in contemporary literature Genet's criminality exemplifies the doctrine. Perversion, defined as any act or practice or viewpoint which subverts procreation in the physical sense, is esteemed as a gesture of freedom, in that it negates the creative-procreative impulse. In perversion, the negation of "the creative" becomes literal—an acting out of a more fundamental negation; an example of this is the murder which Caligula attempts when faced with the knowledge that "men die and they are not happy" (Camus, *Caligula*). In this, murder is the ultimate negation, for it genuinely devolves a thing from a human being.

When one can accept the unchanging definitive statement "men die and they are not happy," the indifference of the universe is inescapable. Man dies because the human condition both wills it and allows it. The definitive act of defiance and of superiority over the human condition is to defeat Nature with her own weapon, is to bring about death at will (truly, one's *last will*).

Hence, for the protagonist of *Steps* suicide is an act stemming out of the present. In performing suicide a man chooses to escape from his future and from his past, thus overcoming the knowledge that he will die.

Suicide implies taking over a natural function. To die in nature's time is to accede to a denial of man's dignity: to die in one's own time is to affirm that dignity. Suicide proves man's power to choose—his final act, if nothing else. The possibility of such choice comforts him in the face of the predictable.

In committing suicide, the man makes himself historical (that is, people can and must preface their statements about him with "he was"). He is transferring the burden of his past onto the shoulders of the world, onto history.

But even in self-destruction, his shadow outlives him. He imposes on other people the necessity for remembering and for judging him, for summarizing him as a character. He creates the means to outlive himself.

Sade's vision is theatrical because, from the outset, he reduces the other person to most basic characteristics. To others, he depicts only those facets of their character which advance his own intended action. Sade *behaves in scenes* (behaves, as opposed to acting out and even to acting), each scene evolving toward its own specific result. The other person, then, becomes a function of his purpose. Automatically, the other person is the stage onto which Sade also automatically projects a cast taken from his own past. Only in this way can he act out his self; only by such means can he obtain a kind of purgation derived from the scene which does not last beyond the scene's physical duration. Thus Sade must act again and again—without lasting satisfaction, without the true recognition of having discarded the forms of his past. In forcing history to summarize him in a word, he has obliterated his self, but has marked his survivors with chosen forms of his past, with his particular shadow.

For the protagonist of *Steps* memories carry no emotions: they exist as incidents, as concise dramas. He does not remember (*i.e.*, experience) his past emotion or pain. He can recall his response to a specific incident in the past—a movement of the mind, a physical reaction—but he cannot reexperience the pain or the emotion proper which produced this response.

For the protagonist of *Steps* emotions have no memories; they exist only in the present. When he reads emotion into memory, he is acting in the present, spontaneously filling in the structures of the drama with feeling (this is similar to what one does when engrossed in a play or in music). Thus he is revisiting the present.

A speculative aside: memories have no emotions, and emotions have no memories. Perhaps that is why the Nazis were compelled to create emotive memories in order to hold the German people within the strictures of the past and make spontaneous present action impossible. Their purpose was to create a crippled group past and maintain it in an almost frozen state.

A direct way to achieve such a situation was to create an emotionally recalled enemy. Such an enemy had to be easily identifiable and have certain stereotyped characteristics, thus heightening the emotions. In purging an "unhealthy" mass element, a nation was really attempting to purge the unhealthy (the unacceptable) in itself. This selected group served as a screen on which one could project one's own individually crippled past. This was acting out a transference.

Does a man's commission of a crime take for granted his commitment of himself to it? Or is guilt a choice after the fact? Does a time come when a man judges himself? What makes a man guilty in his own eyes?

Do the Germans feel guilt? Have they ever chosen to admit to themselves the crimes they committed? The Nazi actions, unlike Meursault's killing of the Arab in *L'Étranger*, were not totally gratuitous: they were planned and carried out, premeditated in the extreme. The case of the Nazis accepting the crime is not merely that of accepting the black humor of an indifferent universe. Bending to the will of a totally gratuitous circumstance is not the same as choosing guilt. If the Germans as a nation accept a communal guilt, as individuals they do not necessarily accept a personal one. Communal guilt still leaves the individual innocent.

Deliberately to choose as a victim an individual or a group with a definable past to eliminate spontaneity from murder surpasses in its impersonality even ritual killing, since it is devoid of emotion. Rational murder is the ultimate anti-theater. Theater implies *agon*, a struggle between two forces; it is essentially two-sided because it depicts the struggle within an intimate relationship. Massacre, then, is also ultimate anti-theater; the Holocaust (one-sided horror) is contrary to truly emotional killing.

Whereas ritual murder at least implies the superiority of the murderer—the priority of the persecutor over the persecuted—mass murder on the scale of the Holocaust dissolves this distinction in the bureaucracy. Bureaucracy entails levels of routine, duties to be performed, patterns which preclude passion. Hannah Arendt's term "the banality of evil" is apt; mass acting out is usually devoid of drama.

When the nameless boy in *Steps* kills the peasant children, he enters a drama of a relationship with a stranger. He selects only those facets of the individual which suit his action. Hence his victims are never personalities but characters, pure attributes. They are the means to an end, and (as the boy perceives them) they carry that end in themselves. They are children of certain parents—indispensable to him because they can be killed and because their deaths will produce the desired effect on both the killer and the parents. They are simply the instruments of revenge, not intimately enough involved with the boy to make their murder a crime of passion. They serve a specific purpose, however; the crime defines them lucidly enough to make their deaths take on the character of ritual murder.

Perhaps these murders satisfy the murderer's sense of self and gain for him an increased solidity, a temporary freedom, a previously unreachable equality, and at the same time an absolute superiority—delivering sensual abandonment, disguised as rituals of drama. After all, Sade's erotic situations are also ritual acts and dramas. In such moments of condensed awareness of life, the boundaries between acting and acting out are constantly being obliterated. What follows is, in *Steps*, a sense of the protagonist's total freedom—and his opposition to the total state.

Shakespeare's works can be cited and recited here. For instance, Iago's actions upon Othello, although they seem simple compared with the complex murder they provoke, make him an equal of the Moor, and ultimately his superior. His actions force Othello to bear Iago's forms of the past so completely that the

Moor identifies himself with Iago. Iago has estranged himself
from the relationship; he has projected himself so wholly upon
the Moor that, although the play in the early stages is about
Iago, the later stages are about Othello, who has adopted Iago's
persona.

Murder is an act of intimacy, a potent bond between killer and
victim in which the killer, at the moment of the act, by facing
the victim's capitulation establishes his own superiority—a superiority over life, until that moment the most superior force of
all. In literal murder, as well as in the symbolic killing of the
other in an intimate relationship, the act of murder is an act of
total commitment, and the very instant the deed is done, the
murderer acknowledges his withdrawal in the purest sense.

In the symbiotic relationship, subject and object are mutually
dependent and sadistic-masochistic roles are interchanged.
Commedia Erudite treated the master-servant relation as comic,
introducing the clever servant who leads his master by the nose
and directs the machinations of the intrigue. The *Commedia
dell'Arte* carries this inversion further, making Harlequin the
hero while Pantaleone, the master, is cast as the fool. In Elizabe-
than and French neoclassic drama the servant or the parasite
drains and subjects the master. Today, the basis of horror is
often the theft of the self, the fear of having one's identity
overshadowed. This is most frightening when in the symbiotic
relationship the thief is the former object—the employee, the
servant, the outcast, the intruder from a lower class.

Sadomasochism implies a lack of acknowledgment of the self
by the other. This relation, more than hate, is the true opposite
of love, for if love is the dual acknowledgment of two selves,
sadomasochism denies them totally. In *Steps*, in the incident of

the man who possesses a woman without her knowing who he is, her making love to him disaffirms his very self.

Contemporary writers often portray the temptation of self-denial in the symbol of bourgeois man tantalized by the prospects of self-surrender and his craving for ritual situations. In their view the bourgeois self is so caught up in abstract existence, so barely possessed of itself, so diseased, that it is continually tempted to relinquish itself altogether and to let the remnants of its social awareness wither away. Large segments of Western literature are devoted to varied forms of malaise. The disease motif in a contemporary work is often built up around a wasting illness— like consumption, as is the case in *Steps*. For Camus a plague symbolizes sickness of society. Sartre declares that nausea, a preliminary to disease, is the only possible response to the contingencies of life. The dwarfishness and the deformity of Günter Grass's narrator in *The Tin Drum* make palpable the angst and spiritual malaise of society sickened by it all in which he lives. And the fictional–nonfictional violence of so many contemporary American novels gives access to the dark desires, the fantasies and the frustration that live just below the polished urban or suburban surface.

In *Steps*, the sanatorium episode profiles the curious symbolic mating of the professionally healthy (the ski instructors) and the chronically unhealthy (the tubercular patients). In embracing the diseased, the instructors embrace the primordial human predicament. They manifest the intrinsic relationship of the erotic and the heinous, of sex and death.

Hence the motivation of the ski instructors is basically sadistic and that of the patients is masochistic. However, within the act, the ski instructors are subjected to loving the sick who, in the very act of love, can poison them with the then-incurable TB. The ski instructors understand—they recognize the object and define the functions to be performed. But they understand little of love, which, one supposes, attempts to be simultane- ously subject and object, and is the willing relinquishment of the single subject to a new subject created from two single ones, each subject enhanced into one heightened self.

The judge-penitent in Camus' *La Chute* acts out perfectly the sadomasochistic fantasy: only those who have sinned against themselves are qualified to pronounce judgment. For once the sin against the self is recognized as such, once the sin is objectified and ceases to be an intrinsic and inseparable part of the self, one has chosen in favor of the self, made a judgment, and chosen, as in Sartre, for all men. Making the judgment of sin is the one possible way of becoming a judge. As in the Book of Job: "I only am escaped alone to tell thee." Thus the judgepenitent becomes the high priest of the self, of the fulfilled individuality. Thus Sade is perceiving the sins he had committed against himself for others' benefit and decides to live fully as himself, for himself, and can therefore preach the doctrine of the judge-penitent.

An obsession is a compulsive self's love affair with itself. The bond is strongly erotic; obsessions—vice, alcoholism, compulsive eating, drug addiction, etc.—all provide their victims with sensual pleasure. Rilke wrote: "To be loved means to be consumed. To love is to give light with inexhaustible oil. To be loved is to pass away. To love is to endure." These maxims apply perfectly to the obsessed and to their obsessions. In the archetypal religious obsessions—the mystic's craving for God, the cases of diabolical possession—the obsessions are expressed in openly sexual imagery and visions take on direct or symbolic sexual forms.

TIME OF LIFE, TIME OF ART

To the photographer in the *Steps*, compulsively guided by his inner sexual camera obscura, the nurse is an image of youth and purity. To her, he is a thing; he possesses the limited function of an object, interchangeable with another object performing the same function, with the atavistic creature she tends. The photographer is the thing which completes her gesture. But since he has created her, in the sense of creating an image of her, she is as much a part of his self, as much in control of him, as alcoholism is of an alcoholic. And so in his submission to this obsession he becomes an object.

In admitting his obsession, an addict is objectifying it, separating himself from it, and is thus able to comment upon it and upon its relationship to himself. Since the self is in the superior position of commenting upon its involvements, the obsession no longer objectifies the self. The addict can then choose and does choose, in pronouncing for or against continuing his involvement with the obsession. The obsession thus becomes a thing.

In *Steps* the incident of the caged woman (anything but incidental in the context of this story about a man caged by his very self) is ordered by a progression of images from the literal cage to the legal cage to the religious cage. The priest is imprisoned in the conflict arising between the systems imposed on him. The woman's madness is also a cage, as is her being set aside by the village, her relegation to a secret place.

The treatment by the villagers of the woman in the cage is the communal acting out of an obsession. To primitive people, feelings and obsessions—of anguish and fear—can be personified and acted out on a social level in dances, ritual, religion.

The men who visit and possess the caged woman are visiting and possessing her in order to fulfill the fantasies of their very obsessions as much as in order to have them released. And as is the case with a ritual, they function in partial secrecy; they are the interpreters of the mystery, the hierophants; they are superior, they are the chosen few.

It is ironic that the woman is unbaptized and thus excluded from the Church. Ironic, because confronting her predicament the priest is obviously confronted here with rituals older than religion.

"Hell is other people" (Sartre). Hell is the inability to escape from others who prove and prove again to you that you are as they see you. Hell is also the inability to be alone, to see yourself as your self sees you. Both convert the subjectivity of the other into a menacing object and originate the sadomasochistic struggle to impose our will upon the Other more dominantly than the Other can impose his or her will on us. At stake is the retention of the dominant position. This enables one to pronounce judgment, for only the subject can judge; the object can only be chosen. To choose is to manifest individuality, even when the alternatives are externally or gratuitously imposed, as in Camus' *L'Étranger*. Meursault murders by chance, but he learns he must choose murdering as a form of expression, must embrace his condition and live it fully. So he hopes the crowd will jeer and spit at him when he is executed—he will have fulfilled himself.

In a time of crumbling systems the protagonist of *Steps* searches for symbols and finds that what is offered him is paper-thin. Pushing against them, he resembles a clown jumping through paper hoops. Thrown back on himself and spared the chilly comfort of power structures, he seeks traditions and finds only his own brief heritages, those which he had experienced in an instant and will retain all his life. But this wisdom mocks his courage.

And his own traditions, he soon learns, are only sensory recollections, fragments of events, and his personality is a kaleidoscope in which the same reflecting specks appear again and again, but in such different patterns that he himself rarely recognizes them. The whole of his legacy is his consciousness, the fiction which begins and ends with itself. And the stories he tells: how can any of them be autobiographical, or less than that? But how can it be autobiographical when he possesses only a bare sense of himself, and when that sense is only perceptible as the most subtle of nuances lurking beneath the reality in which he believes he lives?

For him, to reach back through a particularly painful past for an age of innocence, for the self which, he feels, is waiting for discovery behind the blocked memories preceding his traumas, is to immerse himself in the heart of the trauma itself. To discard forgetting is to be harrowed by the past; it is to expose raw nerve ends and disrupt the benign haziness of present memories. This process, for instance, when it is channeled into a narrative arouses in the hearer a response similar to that evoked by action-painting: an identification with the aspects of personality strewn and spattered throughout the story. In *Steps* the protagonist comes across as an aggregate of memory and emotion which mark and score the novel. Characters and events stand not so much as figurations in a fictive reality but rather as stimuli triggering a hyper-personal, hyper-psychic series of responses in the reader.

Psychoanalysis claims to be able to examine the crippled past in the context of the present in order to frame that past more clearly and thus create a more comprehensible present. This is evasion. It considers the present as a function of the past and

of the future—not as an independent entity. It supposes that
we require being reminded.

We speak of a comic vision or a tragic vision, but being tragic
is not the property of the world in which the artist lives but
rather of the world he creates—of those fragments of experience
he selects without conscious choice, of the self he chooses to
bring up. Certainly, even in life, incidents are sad or funny.
The comic exists really, as does the disastrous. But life is not
so pure as to lay down incident after incident in a single vein;
life has no structure, only frontiers. But a work of art can be
funny or sad, hopeful or tragic, and its structure offers a point
of entry into life—its structure, not merely its content.

There is a kind of grotesque—that of dreams and surrealism—
in which symbols rationally unrelated in subject, tone and emotional content are lured together into a collage which the mind
comprehends on a subconscious level. Here again the work
produces in us responses we cannot normally summon up; the
aroused emotions take us by surprise, bringing to the surface
truths which lie beneath.

Displacing particular images, shifting them into contexts
with which they are not normally associated, makes us aware
of another reality in the midst of our commonplace one. Bosch
was a master of this kind of grotesque. By placing sexual scenes
in religious settings and *vice versa* he displayed the exaggerated,
the twisted, the strange subconscious links which bind the
mind. The result is a dreamlike, nightmarish reality which
shocks, astonishes, and is easily accessible. In truth, its familiarity and its power to stun are fused. The grotesque is the
language of the emotions which silently provoke our actions.
Hence the subversive quality of art.

Art is an autonomous reality. A work of art governs its own time, which is always in play with the external flow of time provided by the spectator. The literary image implies a domination of the dimensions, of empirical space-time, which is impossible in life as we live it. In Wilde's *The Picture of Dorian Gray* the time of art and the time of life are reversed—the portrait ages, the living subject of the portrait does not and instead obeys artistic time, never aging, never changing. The *avant-garde* attempts to acquire a sense of time and of self in which past, present and future are nearly simultaneous. It suggests that novelty depends on spontaneity, the element of unfamiliarity, of surprise. Surprise is instantaneous, and the familiar is the habitual. Habit and routine are stultifying and the *avant-garde* seeks an acknowledgment that art and life have changed places: when our lives are too "real" (mundane, ordered, predictable), we seek excitement and release in fiction. Now, the *avant-garde* claims, due to our so chancy existence, our lives become themselves like fictions—hence literature, graphic art, the cinema must supply the truly real, truly felt experience. This is a phenomenon of mass culture, along with ubiquitous reportage aiming for spontaneity (which nonetheless becomes history the moment it appears in print) for an "objective" fact-based fiction. But fiction is nothing else but the enacted fantasy, the imagination's own form.

Natural symbolism presupposes the omnipotence of nature and is a throwback to a primitive period when man existed in a more direct relationship with nature. The world was alive with magical presences then, and the gods were immanent in natural forces—in the sun and in the trees and in the stones. This was a period preceding organized religion (if religion means approaching the otherwise unapproachable, and marks the moment when the gods or god became supernatural).

In the prereligious period man existed as an inseparable unit of community in the face of nature; the awareness of himself as an individual did not ensue. It is only when the gods begin to grow distant and earth and heaven become separate worlds that the concept of the self arises.

The feeling of magic, the sense of community, the euphoric sense of belonging to others rather than to oneself, all can be conjured up, and nature as incantation still survives. Natural symbolism invokes incantatory nature and serves for a moment to create a community response, producing a sense which antedates the individual response.

Natural symbolism also employs macrocosmic analogies. Incantatory nature is mystical, omnipotent, something unknown and sacred. When a natural analogy is made, the thing compared is immeasurably strengthened; it becomes microcosm.

With the birth of collective and mechanized society, faith loses its meaning. In the face of faith lost and in a universe unmasked in its indifference, collective values must be enforced as the true representatives of belief. But these collective values are mementos of the god-fearing society, and they weigh on the individual. The protagonist of *Steps* is aware of this and to him the most meaningful and fulfilling gesture is negative; aimed against the collective it brings about the solitude within which the self can display its reality. Perhaps that is why the nameless persona of this novel looks for the true gesture outside society, at the edge of despair, turning more and more often for inspiration to the outsider, to the pariah, to his own journey in *Steps*.

Centuries before Freud, Sophocles pictured the human effort to unify the unconscious and conscious, but in *Oedipus* the only blocks against regression are external. History moves inward; the struggles that occur between the external and the internal move inward. Modern art becomes hyper-personal or else repeats its familiar disinterested message in the undercharged but accessible images of universal misery, desperately trying to express the individual's difficulty in systematically functioning in a rigidly imposed system.

Jung suggests that there had once been a wholeness of the conscious and the unconscious, a unification of public and private appearances. Although Jung is referring to a primordial mentality, to a naïve abundance of involvuntary thought, we find this unity most vividly symbolized in the arts preceding the Jacobean period. When this unity occurs, myth is potent and tragedy takes place. Claiming that tragedy imitates an action, Aristotle implies this wholeness. Today, with the public mask and private action dissociated, the period of synthesis in art emerges as not distant. Meanwhile, neurosis has replaced the myth. This is why so much of modern fiction bears a certain universality, an allegorical intent: the collective consciousness and any individual collection of consciousness have been radically detached. Jung's definition of the use of myth as a type of self-therapy is easily corroborated in modern fiction, which abounds in myths and reworked classical motifs. The purpose of these motifs is thus not so gratuitous as it seems.

When creation falls from the active to the gestural mode, it exhibits a resurgence of mythic motifs, which, like incantations, are an attempt to reassemble the last active unity. But it often achieves only a Pavlovian response, the true opposite of the primal spontaneity.

The myth and the ritual serve a structural rather than an active function. Literature has preempted the functions of both. But myths—even dead and moribund ones—still have evocative power and still exist in our thoughts. As tradition is continually attacked in art, myths exist to be broken. Literature seeks to describe what is, and, in the process, to do away with what is not or what is no longer.

From this function of literature arises the necessity for the subversive, for subversion makes its points by indirection; the most seductive and insinuating attack is the indirect one. Formerly, the wanderer returned home safely, wiser from what he had learned in his journeys. Now the wanderer returns safely, but his wisdom is disquieting and he has only affirmed what he has all along suspected. He discovers that his quest in search of inner life is a symbol for something lost or untouched by him. The modern wanderer travels in an empty universe as solitary as that which lies behind his own self: ". . . I would have stayed in my seat with my eyes closed, all strength and passion gone, my mind as quiescent as a coat rack under a forgotten hat, and I would have remained there, timeless, unmeasured, unjudged, bothering no one, suspended forever between my past and my future." (*Steps*)

1968

AFTERWORDS

D I S G U I S E S *

Jerzy Kosinski killed himself on May third: I was among his admirers. His penchant for disguises was well known, and the current issue of *Vanity Fair* (October 1991) publishes color photos of Kosinski variously camouflaged. It reminded me of a talk we had at NBC some years ago about his proclivity. It was just after the publication of his novel *Pinball*. I have transcribed this exactly, only adding commas to indicate the pauses and cadence of his extremely rapid Polish-accented speech.

K: I've had some thoughts about wearing a disguise. What happened recently—actually it's rather sad—I go to Latin America very often where I like to play polo. In one particular country where I play polo quite often, about eleven miles away from the polo grounds there's a small industrial town. Now, there are no mysteries in Poland for me anymore, but many in the little town. And so, over the years, I would go there to the little town, and since I'm not Latin, and I would like to be Latin, I pretended I was deaf-mute. I really didn't lie. I don't

*From an interview with Gene Shalit, 1980.

speak Spanish, which means I'm mute. And I don't understand Spanish, which means I'm deaf. I acknowledged this by becoming deaf-mute. Over the years I developed friendships with the local people, who knew me only as a deaf-mute, a Latin. They thought I was from another town, and I would come with my limited funds. Nevertheless, given the dimension of this small, poor town, I was a rich deaf-mute, Latin. And among those who befriended me was a local man, a thirty-year-old, a man whose name was Henry. He was my guide and my friend and he would take me around and apologize for my being deaf-mute. And he would say, "He's nice. This guy, he can write if you ask questions." I can write some Spanish, so I can answer questions. There's no accent when you write. And it worked very well and I would go out nights with a great sense of adventure. There I was living a life of a Latin, in a small, poor, Latin town. Many things happen in that way. New York is a Latin town as well, so you know. And then *Reds* [the movie] hit the screens in the United States. And my new novel was about to be published. And I was interviewed by a local paper [where he played polo] and I didn't think about it. They came, they photographed me as a polo player living among rich Americans. Eleven miles away was a town where nobody knew I was a novelist, nobody knew I was a movie star, quote unquote, nobody knew I was someone else. And I didn't think about it. And three days later, in a local paper called *Ultima Hora—The Latest Hour—* there was a picture of an American of Polish origin, Jerzy Kosinski, an author, a movie star—and a fraud. Eleven miles away they didn't know about it. And when I got the paper I suddenly realized that I had done something absolutely awful, so that night, as I had done many times before, I took my car to the little town to see Henry—that's the guy—and his friends. And they had *Ultima Hora* in their hands, and they wouldn't talk to me. And they said, "You are the most disgusting man around," and they said it in English. And I said, "Where's Henry? Let me explain." I said, "I really didn't lie to him. I'm not Latin, but I'm a human being, and by not speaking to all of you I was much more part of you than I would have been had I spoken my brand of English." They said, "You lied. You're not a man, you're a *liar*. You're just a liar. You go ahead and write your American novels." And I said, "Where's Henry?" And they said, "Henry. Henry did something awful last night when he read *Ultima Hora*." I said, "What did he do?" Well, Henry went berserk. And in the act of becoming berserk, he lost face. His friend was—a fraud. And Henry committed a crime. And was arrested and went to prison. I contributed to the defense fund, but Henry was destroyed by my—well, publicity if you want. And that's basically what *Pinball* was about, but when I was writing *Pinball* I didn't think about consequences of this sort, and now I do, and I don't think I'm going to wear disguises as often as, as I used to.

1980

ON DEATH

I am gazing at death, which is non-presence. There is no question about death being a part of life, but not death in a gas chamber. Nor at a concentration camp. There is nothing more detrimental to vision than the ashes of each person which, it used to be said, were worth nine German marks. Here you have a culture reduced not just to non-presence, not even to a secondary presence, but to ashes. This is a vision that endangers our place in the chamber of history. One must bow to every single death and say: What a pity you are not here. We are very sorry you died this way. Think, all of you, the living, how much those dead could have done for us, for the whole class learning history. Think of all the inventions, all the books, all the ideas! Think of what has been lost in that horrible place that should be called, of all things, a chamber. . . .

1989

SOURCES

"Motto" from interview by Lisa Grunwald in *Vineyard Gazette*, Martha's Vineyard, July 29, 1977.

Reflections on Life and Death
"Aleksander and André Wat," adapted from conversations and lectures, August 1989.
"Time to Spare," *New York Times* Op Ed, May 21, 1979. Copyright ©1979 by Jerzy Kosinski.
"Death in Cannes," *Esquire*, Vol. 105, No. 3, March 1986.

Life and Art
"On Books," 1989. Copyright © 1989 by Jerzy Kosinski.
"To Touch Minds," adapted from conversations and lectures, August 11, 1989.
"The Reality Behind Words," *New York Times* Op Ed, October 3, 1971.
"Where an Author Can Be Himself," 1969 National Book Award acceptance speech.
"Our 'Predigested, Prepackaged Pop Culture'—A Novelist's View," from an interview in *U.S. News & World Report*, January 8, 1979.
"To Hold a Pen," *The American Scholar*, Vol. 42. No. 4, Autumn 1973.

"A Sense of Place," from P.E.N./Faulkner Awards talk, October 1, 1990. Copyright © 1990 by Jerzy Kosinski.

"My Twenty-Minute Performance," adapted from an interview with Jeff Reid in *Minnesota Daily*, Vol. 83, No. 142. April 9, 1982.

"On Journalists: Combining Objective Data with Subjective Attitudes," *Bulletin of the American Society of Newspaper Editors*, July/August 1981.

Artists and Eye

"On Sculpture: Sculptorids of Rhonda Roland Shearer." Foreword to the catalogue for Rhonda Roland Shearer exhibition, Wildenstein Gallery, October 17–November 9, 1990.

"Photography as Art," *American Photographer*, Vol. IV, No. 6, June 1980.

"On Film and Literature," December 17, 1977.

The Sporty Self

"How I Learned to Levitate in Water," *Life*, Vol. 7, No. 4, April 1984.

"Crans-Montana—The Open Resort" combined from *New York Times*, Travel: Special Ski Issue, November 1, 1981: "In Search of the Perfect Slope," and *Crans-Montana Sporting Life*, Winter 1983: "The Plaine-morte." Copyright © 1983 by Jerzy Kosinski.

"Horses," *Centaur*, Summer I 1981. Copyright © 1981 by Jerzy Kosinski.

"A Passion for Polo," *Polo*, Vol. 11, No. 1, May 1985.

Talk of New York

"New York: The Literary Autofocus," from an essay on photography, April 5, 1991. Copyright © 1991 by Jerzy Kosinski.

"Key to New York," *Paris Match*, May 1979. Copyright © 1979 by Jerzy Kosinski.

"Time Machine," *New York* magazine, December 24–31, 1990.

Short Takes
"Manhattan," November 1981
"A Celebration of Literacy and Learning," from *The New York Public Library*, October 12, 1989.
"Gotham Book Mart," tribute to Frances Steloff, 1987. Copyright 1987 by Jerzy Kosinski.
"New York Is a City of Port and Sport," *New York* magazine, December 24–31, 1984.
"Beach Wear," *Vanity Fair*, April 8, 1985.
"Being Here," *New York* magazine, May 12, 1986.

People, Places and Me
"Charisma Camouflages Mortality," New York *Daily News*, May 14, 1981.
"Solzhenitsyn: The Disenchanted Pilgrim" (answer to "Is Solzhenitsyn Right?" in Nation section), *Time*, June 26, 1978, and from "Predigested . . ." in *U.S. News & World Report*, January 8, 1979.
"A Message to the Chamber from Jerzy Kosinski," from "Spanish/U.S. Chamber of Commerce 27th Anniversary Salutes the European Community," New York 1986. Copyright © 1986 by Jerzy Kosinski.
"A Brave Man, This Beatty. Brave As John Reed . . ." *Vogue*, April 1982.
"Egypt, Polo and the Perplexed I," *Polo* magazine, 1989.
"A Plea to Khomeini from an Author Whose Work Also Has Offended," *The World Paper*, 1989.

Self vs. Collective
"Gog and Magog: On watching TV," *Time*, March 6, 1990.
"TV as Baby-Sitter" (revised November 1989), from NBC-TV comment, September 3, 1972. Copyright © 1972 by Jerzy Kosinski.
"Against Book Censorship," *Media & Methods*, January 1976. Copyright © 1976 by Jerzy Kosinski.
"Dead Souls on Campus," *New York Times* Op Ed, October 13, 1970.
"The Banned Book as Psychological Drug—A Parody?" *Media & Methods*, January © 1977. Copyright © 1977 by Jerzy Kosinski.

Jewish Presence

Foreword to *No Religion Is an Island*, a collection of essays on Rabbi Heschel, edited by Byron L. Sherwin and Harold Kosimow. Mary Knoll, N.Y.: Orbis Books, 1991.

"*God &. . . ,*" contributed chapter to *God &. . .* , by Terrance A. Sweeney. Minneapolis: Winston Press, 1985.

"Jews in the Soviet Union," November 25, 1981.

"Hosanna to What?" *Boston Sunday Globe*, Focus, November 4, 1990 (published title "The Second Holocaust").

"Restoring a Polish-Jewish Soul," *New York Times* Op Ed, October 22, 1988.

"Speaking for My Self," *Dialectics & Humanism*, No.1, 1987. Copyright © 1987 by Jerzy Kosinski.

Time of Life, Time of Art

"Afterward: *The Painted Bird* 10th Anniversary Edition," Houghton Mifflin, 1976. Copyright © 1976 by Jerzy Kosinski.

"Notes of the Author on *The Painted Bird*," Scientia-Factum, 1965. Copyright © 1965 by Jerzy N. Kosinski.

"The Art of the Self: Essays à propos *Steps*," Scientia-Factum, 1969. Copyright © 1968 by Jerzy Kosinski.

Afterwords

"Disguises," *Shalit's Sampler*, October 1991 (from an interview with Gene Shalit on NBC January 1980).

"On Death," adapted from conversations and lectures, 1989.

Born on June 14, 1933, of Mieczyslaw and Elzbieta Kosinski in Lodz, Poland, JERZY KOSINSKI came to the United States in 1957. He was naturalized in 1965. Mr. Kosinski obtained M.A. degress in social sciences and history from the University of Lodz, and as a Ford Foundation Fellow completed his postgraduate studies in sociology at both the Polish Academy of Sciences in Warsaw and Columbia University in New York. He wrote *The Future is Ours, Comrade* (1960) and *No Third Path* (1962), both collections of essays he published under the pen name of Joseph Novak. He is the author of the novels *The Painted Bird* (1965), *Steps* (1968), *Being There* (1971), *The Devil Tree* (first edition 1973, revised in 1981), *Cockpit* (1975), *Blind Date* (1977), *Passion Play* (1979), *Pinball* (1982) and *The Hermit of 69th Street* (1988).

As a Guggenheim Fellow, Mr. Kosinski studied at the Center for Advanced Studies at Wesleyan University; subsequently he taught American prose at Princeton and Yale universities. He then served the maximum two terms as president of the American Center of P.E.N., the international association of writers and editors. He was also a Fellow of Timothy Dwight College at Yale University. Mr. Kosinski founded and served as president of the Jewish Presence Foundation, based in New York.

Mr. Kosinski won the National Book Award for *Steps*, the American Academy of Arts and Letters Award in literature, best Screenplay of the Year Award for *Being There* from both the Writers Guild of America and the British Academy of Film and Television Arts (BAFTA), the B'rith Shalom Humanitarian Freedom Award, the Polonia Media Award, the American Civil Liberties Union First Amendment Award and International House Harry Edmonds Life Achievement Award. He was a recipient of honorary Ph.D.s in Hebrew letters from Spertus College of Judaica and in humane letters from both Albion College, Michigan (1988) and Potsdam College of New York State University (1989).

An adept of photographic art, with one-man exhibitions to his credit in Warsaw's State Crooked Circle Gallery (1957), André Zarre Gallery in New York (1988) and in the Spertus College of Judaica in Chicago (1992), Mr. Kosinski was also an avid polo player and skier. In his film-acting debut in Warren Beatty's *Reds*, he portrayed Grigori Zinoviev, the Russian revolutionary leader.

Mr. Kosinski died in New York on May 3, 1991.